A Woman's Work

Riade MacMillan .

A Woman's Work

CHANGING CHRISTIAN ATTITUDES

Anne Borrowdale

First published in Great Britain 1989
SPCK
Holy Trinity Church
Marylebone Road
London NW1 4DU

Acknowledgements

The illustrations by Posy Simmonds are reprinted
by permission of the Peters, Fraser and Dunlop Group Ltd.

British Library Cataloguing in Publication Data

Borrowdale. Anne
  A Woman's Work
  1. Great Britain. Woman., Employment – Christian viewpoint
  I. Title
261.8'5
ISBN 0-281-04399-X

Typeset by Studio 21
Printed in Great Britain by
Anchor Press, Tiptree

Contents

Introduction

Women constitute half the world's population, perform nearly two-thirds of its work hours, receive one tenth of the world's income and own less than one hundredth of the world's property.[1]

A woman will always sacrifice herself if you give her the opportunity. It is her favourite form of self-indulgence.[2]

Christians ought to know a great deal about love and service. It is central to our faith that Christ sacrificed himself for us, and that we ought to sacrifice ourselves in the service of others for his sake. Sunday by Sunday in church, we are encouraged to put the needs of others before our own, and to give without counting the cost or seeking a reward.

Women know a great deal about love and service. Across the world they are responsible for the daily nurturing of men and children, both within their own families and in society at large. They are constantly required to put other people's needs before their own, and to find fulfilment in a life of sacrificial service.

Is there any connection between these two things? Certainly Christianity attracts large numbers of women. In industrialized nations at least, the majority of church attenders are female, and religion plays an important part in many women's lives. Women who are not regular churchgoers often value the religious dimension of events such as weddings and christenings. The fact that many women's lives consist of serving others in the way advocated by Christianity surely does have significance. But is it that women are religious and serve others because they are *better* than men – the 'naturally nicer sex'? Or is it their religious beliefs which prompt them into a life of virtue? Or is the connection a more subtle one? Perhaps women's readiness to serve others contributes to their oppression and is sometimes harmful, but the fact that it looks so much like Christian service prevents the problems associated with it from being recognized. This book is an exploration of these questions.

There are numerous Christian books which examine what it means to live as a Christian, and which examine work theologically. What

1

these books generally lack is a focus on women's experience, and on the fact that service has a particular association with femininity. For example, in the theology of work, 'work' is usually equated with paid employment, so that the high proportion of women's work which is unpaid and in the home is hardly considered at all.

There are many other books which discuss the role Christian women should play in Church and society. Most suggest that women's primary calling is to be wives and mothers – and are somewhat unsatisfactory in their treatment of women who are not in these roles. Such books may contain sensible advice on running a home and managing relationships with husband and children. Since most are written by women, they do reflect many of women's daily concerns. But whilst these things are set in the context of a relationship with God, the theological implications of women's service are not thought through.

In a world where so much is changing, many women are unsure about what being female means, and look for direction and reassurance. Books which tell them that they are very special creatures in God's eyes, with a unique, divinely ordained role to play are extremely popular among Christian women; they fill a need to know how to behave in today's world. I used to read such material myself whilst a young, single woman, anxious to discover how to be properly and Christianly feminine and attract the right mate. I am now relieved that my period of quiet, submissive femininity did not last long, but I know what it feels like to believe in a rather restricted form of Christian womanhood.

Although there might seem to be a world of difference between those who believe in women's subordination and Christian feminists, they in fact share many of the same concerns. Both groups are interested in how women are treated in employment, relationships in the family, and sexism in the Church. Some evangelicals like Anne Atkins and Elaine Storkey find they can adopt a feminist position.[3] Christian women also have a common commitment to loving and serving God and others aright, and I have tried to build on that shared concern in this book.

In order to explore the connections between Christianity, service and women's lives, we need both a proper theological critique and a real understanding of women's experience. Much of the Christian discussion about women has focused on what women should or should not do in the Church, and on what role men and women should play in marriage. These debates can be a way of looking at important theological questions about God and what it means to be human. But there is a danger that discussions of 'women in Church and society' simply recycle stale arguments, and take us nowhere. I have therefore tried to come in at a different point, by starting with women's experience rather than the Bible and Christian tradition, although my Christian reflection is based on these things.

Inevitably there are limitations in a book of this size, given the vast amount of material which is relevant to women's experience. I have not been able to present a global picture of women's service, although that perspective would have enriched and widened the scope of my material. Because I am the mother of small children, I am especially interested in how Christian service relates to motherhood, and this is reflected in what I have written. But I have also focused on other areas of women's lives, such as older women who are carers, single women, and the different jobs which women do. I have not included a great many statistics about women's employment, or reproduced much material where women speak directly of their lives, for these are widely available elsewhere. I have indicated some of these sources, however, in the Notes.

The main focus of this book is the service women perform, not because men do not serve others, but because service is particularly attached to the feminine role. However, there are parallels between the situation of male ministers and women's caring role, and men will relate to some of the issues surrounding service for women, even if these do not affect them in quite the same way.

Much of this book arose out of the research I did for my Ph.D. thesis, completed in 1988 and funded by a grant from the University of Durham. I am grateful to the many friends who discussed my ideas as I went along. In particular, I would like to thank Rosemary Dawson, Elizabeth Nash, Hilary Cashman and my sister Jan Payne for their comments and help during the writing process. Needless to say, any faults in the final product are entirely my own.

Chapter 1

When he walks through that door

To be pleasing to his sight, to win his respect and love, to train him in childhood, to tend him in manhood, to counsel and console, to make his life pleasant and happy, these are the duties of woman for all time.[1]

Women are always being accused of being selfish. All they ask is not always to be the ones who must be unselfish.[2]

There is a curious double standard which operates for men's and women's work. Being at home, looking after small children, preparing meals and feeding the cat is quite easy – as long as it is done by a woman. Doing a day's work in the office or factory is exhausting and stressful – if it is done by a man. But place the man in the home all day and the woman in the office, and a strange transformation takes place. Housework and childcare become mysteriously demanding when a man does them, and employment is the easy option if a woman has chosen it. As in Posy Simmonds' cartoon 'Waiting for Mummy', the woman comes home ready to meet the emotional and physical needs of husband, children, cat and casserole. Any tiredness or stress from her job is presumed to pass before she walks through the door, so that she is immediately available to serve her family's needs.

This pattern is repeated in millions of homes each day, where women who have full-time occupations return to shoulder the major responsibility for household tasks, and for the emotional care of husband and children. They may not do this as graciously as does 'Mummy' in the cartoon, although it is comforting to see that even she gets impatient at the demands of the casserole, but this feeling that they should be constantly ready to put aside their own needs in order to serve others, is a central feature of women's lives.

For most people, the expectation that women will look after men's physical and emotional needs is deeply ingrained. This is most clearly illustrated in the marriage relationship. When a husband comes home from a hard day's work, to a wife who has been at home all day, it is

generally his needs which are to be considered. However stressful a day his wife has had at home, her role is to soothe him and provide a refuge from the demands of his job. This pattern is repeated in millions of homes around the country, when women refrain from unburdening themselves of the frustrations of the day, or keep the children from under the father's feet while he recovers from his work.

The idea that women should service men's needs in marriage is influential even where it is not put into practice very effectively. Wives may come home and complain about their own tiredness, or begin the saga of how awful their day at home has been before their husband has even hung up his coat. But both partners are likely to feel that this is wrong; that wives should put their husbands' feelings first, and that men have the right to a peaceful homecoming. Strictly speaking, this expectation that men's needs must always come first is unjust. Yet few women find it easy to challenge it, because to do so seems to be a denial of love.

In both Christian and secular literature, women are encouraged to give their husbands' needs priority. Alexander Gunn, for example, writing in *Mother and Baby*, asks new mothers:

> Is his tea ready when he comes in, or does he have to wait until the baby's been fed? . . . If you're always tired when he comes home, it's understandable, but a bit boring for him nevertheless to be greeted each evening with a long saga of how exhausting *your* day has been. Is there any chance that you could be anaemic? . . . Is your day really organised so that when your husband comes home in the evening, it is his time for affection and devotion? Of course it sounds as if you have two babies in your life to look after, but then truly you do have – the new one is the tiny one that cries . . undoubtedly a man is a baby at heart, he wants lots of attention too.[3]

Gunn stresses that women must try especially hard to treat men in this way in the first few months after the baby arrives, because it sets the pattern for their lives together. But it is hardly possible for a good adult relationship to be established if men are behaving, and being treated, like babies. Many *Mother and Baby* readers were understandably incensed by this viewpoint, although a minority agreed with it. Gordon Bourne gives similar advice to new mothers in his book on pregnancy: 'Men are sometimes neglected when their wives are pregnant and therefore require just as much attention as a new arrival. Every women should make sure that the new member of the family does not mean that her husband has less of her love, time and affection.'[4]

It may be significant that both Bourne and Gunn are men. Yet women, too, make this point that women's duties are to make life as pleasant as possible for their husbands, and to respond to their every need. It is interesting that several Christian writers point to the importance of how wives treat husbands at tea-time. For Pat King, as for Gunn, a man's tea should be ready when he expects it:

> Our husbands, if we want them to be all that husbands should be, have to be fed as well as possible and on time. . . . Everything else being equal, families who count on dinner on time will have fewer problems and much greater solidarity than families whose dinner is unplanned, vague or haphazard.[5]

Quite what the evidence is for this, I do not know.

King recognizes that this may be hard to do, but any suffering involved is for the sake of Christ:

> Each of us is called by the Lord to holiness. Isn't it amazing that so many of us answer that call through something as everyday as dinner and the dishes? The evening meal is the great paradox of our homemaker lives. It looks . . . so unimportant when we consider all that there is to be done for the cause of Christ. But when we answer this calling to lay down our lives every day at 4.30 with a conscious love for the Lord . . . how can it be anything but important and utterly worthwhile?[6]

If a woman wishes to communicate her feelings to her husband, says James Dobson, she should select the moment when her 'husband is typically more responsive and pleasant . . . The worst time of the day is during the first sixty minutes after he arrives home from work'.[7]

There is some sense in this advice. After all, it *is* helpful for a man to be able to unwind quietly after a hard day's work. The difficulty is not that it is wrong to be sensitive to others, but that it is primarily *woman* who are to be sensitive to *men*. As in Posy Simmonds' cartoon, a woman returning after the rigours of a day's employment rarely receives or expects this kind of consideration. One woman, whose husband does the major share of childcare, reports:

> When I get home at about 5.30, he is practically waiting in the hall with his coat on. He is off out for a quiet drink and a break after the pressures of the day. I don't mind, I know how much more tiring

it is to care for a baby than to do a day's work at the office. Anyway, I enjoy the privacy, being alone with her after so many hours apart.[8]

In the process of ensuring their husbands' needs are met, women's own needs are likely to be shelved or denied. The worst time of day to make demands on a husband may indeed be the first sixty minutes after he arrives home. But this may coincide with the worst time of day for the mother of small children. Worn out by a day filled not only with housework and practical childcare, but also with emotional nurturing and responses, she has to cope with an evening meal and tired, fractious children. This is precisely the moment when she needs someone to be pleasant and responsive to her, to allow her to unwind, or to take over some of the tasks which have to be done. Gunn and Bourne have little appreciation of what it might cost women to act in the way they suggest. King does realize it is hard – she has ten children, and should know! – but makes it difficult for women to object by calling the costs suffering for Christ's sake.

Amongst writers of popular Christian literature about marriage, there are some who do encourage men to help in the house when they come home from work.[9] But for other Christians, the domestic sphere is and should be the woman's responsibility, just as his employment is the man's. Whilst a husband may help occasionally, he should not be *expected* to do so. One Christian man makes an interesting excuse for not being involved in housework and childcare: if fathers wash dishes and bath the baby, sons will not know what it means to be a man; male psychology and physiology are not geared to helping with children.[10] Dobson dislikes 'seeing a man work all day at his job and then be *obligated* to confront his wife's responsibility when he comes home (assuming that she has no outside employment of her own)'. He refers to 'women who have brow-beaten their puppy-dog husbands into cooking and washing dishes every night of the year'. However, he believes that fathers have a role in the management of children, so he might put them to bed or change nappies.[11]

In theory, it might seem reasonable that if a couple agree that the woman does the housework whilst the man earns an income, he should not have to do her 'job' as well as his. But housework may well take more hours a day than the man's employment, particularly if there are children. Is it then fair for a man to expect to relax when he comes home, waited on by a wife who gets no leisure at all? Moreover, it is not always helpful if men are willing to help with childcare but not housework, as Dobson proposes. The two tasks are interrelated, since children need meals and clean clothes as well as games and stories. What men today are showing is increased willingness to take on the more rewarding aspects of childcare, such as playing with children, whilst leaving mothers the tedious routine tasks.

What, then, are the choices open to women when their husbands walk through that door? Should wives be waiting with a coat on to go out for a quiet drink, whilst their husbands take over? Should they thrust the vacuum cleaner, baby or vegetables into their husbands' hands, saying 'You can do this'? What would be the result if they did? Unless they are married to exceptional men, such behaviour is not likely to improve the harmony in the home. Men may attend to household tasks when they come in from work, but do so grudgingly. In any case, if they do not have time to unwind, their tempers may well be short.

It is also an effort for women always to be asking their husbands to contribute. Husbands may say 'You only have to ask' but this perpetuates the idea that men are helping out of kindness, rather than taking on their part of a shared responsibility. One woman remarked that she did not like asking her husband for help, because when she was cross with him for neglecting his share of the housework, she did not want to give him the chance to feel morally superior. Men can feel virtuous as they 'help out', yet women who continually ask men to do things around the house are 'nagging'. The stereotype of the unfeminine, unattractive, nagging wife is a powerful one, and women may prefer to suffer in silence rather than risk being associated with it. To create an issue about who does what in the home can provoke conflict. Since women want their homes to be harmonious, they may keep quiet, even where the situation is unfair.

Some women would face verbal or physical abuse if they did not provide the service that their husbands expect. As Pat King observes when she recommends sacrificial service to wives: 'a happy unthreatened husband who knows he is the head of our house and first in our lives is easy to live with'.[12] It is tempting to suggest that dictators, too, are pleasant to live with, provided their authority is unchallenged and their every wish is met; but that is scarcely a good model for marriage. Nevertheless, many women bite back criticism, bear an unequal load in the house and put their own needs and desires on one side, in order to keep their home free of conflict which might be destructive. Provoking conflict with husbands sours the atmosphere in which women both live and work, and this is particularly hard if they have no escape routes from the home – into employment, or in outside groups.

Women readily admit that they do an unfair proportion of work in the home, but frequently have reasons which justify this in their own situation. Firstly, convincing excuses can be made for husbands who do not help in the home. In a study done by Backett,[13] couples coped with an unfair division of labour by maintaining that husbands *wanted* to do more, and did appreciate the extra work their wives were doing, but the pressures of their jobs prevented them from helping more. They might be doing physically demanding work, or be in stressful jobs, or work unsocial hours. Husbands were said to be unaware of what had to be done, or incompetent at changing nappies or cooking. Many mothers in McKee's survey on father participation in childcare were:

> 'easy' on their husbands, praising their involvement even where it was minimal, accepting reasons for low involvement such as male inexperience, tiredness, disinterest, incompetence, physical unsuitability (clumsiness, large hands), and psychological unsuitability (rough, quick-tempered, impatient, squeamish) – reasons that would not stand up if applied to women.[14]

Couples also looked to the future, when the children would be at different stages, and anticipated fathers doing more then.

Although these excuses appear to be reasonable, the key point is that, as McKee says, none of them would apply to mothers. Women may do hard jobs, but still cope with domestic work. Mothers may relate better to children of a particular age, but cannot opt out of caring for those they find difficult. Many women have never changed a nappy, or are inexperienced at cooking or housework, but they learn to do such tasks because they have to be done. It is true that many men have not learned to look after their own or others' physical needs, but basic maintenance skills are not hard to acquire if the will is there. Men are not really too incompetent to learn, but at times it is convenient for them not to be able to work the washing machine, bath the baby or cook the tea.

Additionally, women may admit that husbands ought to do more but forgive them out of love and readily take on extra burdens for them. If the women are Christians, there is a further motivation to do this. Not only are love and forgiveness proper Christian virtues, but they may feel, with King, that wives must be prepared to put all their energy into the marriage relationship because it is their primary calling. Doing this may look as if it will take them away from what they want for themselves, admits King, but in the end gives them want they *really* want – to be like Christ. Although it may cause women suffering to put 'the plans, the desires and dreams of a husband before (their) . . . own', this suffering is following the example of Christ who laid down his life for them.[15] This may seem to be the proper Christian response, but there are a number of difficulties with it, as I shall indicate.

A third justification for women bearing an unequal proportion of the service load is that it is part of their 'nature' to serve. I shall return to this point in the next chapter.

Excuses of this type can appear to be reasonable; and because it is always much easier not to challenge accepted practice, many women carry on serving despite the cost, and despite the resentment it can engender. As Christians, we have been very ready to stress the importance of service, yet have not always looked at what this means in concrete situations. We have failed to look at the wider implications of women's service for society, and have not seen that a stress on service creates problems for women, and also for those they serve.

Clearly the virtue of service is one which needs to be encouraged. It is not my intention to tell women to stop caring for and about those they love. But somehow we need to discover ways of serving one another which allow all of us to flourish, and do not pit one person's interests against another's. We must rid ourselves of the expectation that *women* will always service *men*, and replace it with an emphasis on mutual understanding and support. We have to find better ways of reflecting in our service and love of others the affirming love of the God whose service is perfect freedom.

Chapter 2

The naturally nicer sex?

Woman is a religion . . . an altar . . . a living poetry that elevates men, raises children, sanctifies the family . . . She will live for others . . . and not for herself . . . Her clear vocation is love . . . She must love and give birth, that is her sacred duty.[1]

Both sexes project those qualities they admire and desire on the opposite sex . . . people glorify these qualities in the opposite sex out of all proportion. Men deny themselves sensitivity and gentleness, but desire these qualities in their women. Women deny themselves assertive and authoritative behavior (*sic*), and demand these qualities of their men.[2]

One reason why women are happy to accept the serving role is that it seems 'natural' for them to care for others. Women are mothers, runs the argument, therefore they have been provided with special nurturing abilities. Certainly caring for others is an integral part of the feminine role, and something in which girls are encouraged from an early age. But a key question is how the caring for others which is supposed to be 'natural' to women, relates to the service which is a principal requirement in the Christian life. Are women 'naturally' saintly or virtuous, as some Christians imply? Are they biologically programmed for servanthood?

For a number of Christian writers, it is indeed in women's 'nature' to serve others, particularly husband and children. Stephen Clark argues at length that God has created 'natural' complementary differences between the sexes which fit them for different roles. Thus he can state that women 'have a natural tendency toward teaching and caring for smaller children and toward certain secretarial positions.'[3] It is interesting to speculate why women might 'naturally' tend toward 'certain secretarial positions'. Perhaps Clark has in mind Luther's point that God made women with 'broad hips and a wide backside to sit upon'![4]

For Pope John Paul II, it is once again women's 'nature' which fits them for a particular role. Fairly sharp general statements about work and justice in the papal encyclical *Laborem Exercens* are strictly limited in their application to women:

> it is fitting that (women) . . . should be able to fulfil their tasks *in accordance with their own nature*, without being discriminated against and without being excluded from jobs for which they are capable, but also without lack of respect for their family aspirations and for their specific role in contributing, together with men, to the good of society. The *true advancement of women* requires that . . . women do not have to pay for their advancement by abandoning what is specific to them.[5]

From their very different theological standpoints, both Pope John Paul II and Clark assume that there is general agreement about the kind of 'nature' women have, and the implications which follow from this. They are clear that women's primary task is within the family, nurturing husband and children, because women have special biological characteristics which fit them for this role. Such a view is widespread, and of course many women do see their primary role as being in the home. But the idea that women's *nature* equips them for serving others is dangerous. It disguises the fact that it is costly for most women to deny themselves in the service of others, and it limits the potential of both sexes to act in ways which do not fit the stereotype.

It might be expected that Christians would be the first to recognize the infinite variety of God's creation, the complexity of human nature and behaviour. Yet many Christians repeat very stereotyped views of masculinity and femininity, and affirm these as God's pattern for humankind. Women are frequently represented as nurturant, sensitive, creative and more spiritually-minded than men. Women's 'nature', said one speaker at a Mission England conference for Christian women, is one of harmony, patience and self-giving. These qualities are balanced by negative ones. Women are also vulnerable, moody, unreasonable and prone to depression, for reasons connected with menstruation and hormone imbalance. Their greater enthusiasm for new ideas means they are more likely to be deceived than are men. Men are often portrayed by Christians as logical, strong, able to lead, technically competent, and aggressive. For one writer, a man has the bent of hostility and aggression, and this 'is part of his, just as creativity is part of woman's, essential being'.[6]

Characteristics such as these are emphasized because they

contribute to a 'package' which superficially makes sense. For example, Brand writes:

> God has made women to be soft-shelled and vulnerable. Yet he did not intend us to live without protection. He meant us to live under the caring shelter of the men he set over us. . . . Within their protection, we can remain fully sensitive, fully responsive, full of bright ideas, flexible and lively, without the danger that comes from this soft-shelled state.[7]

The theory that the sexes have different but complementary qualities and roles is an attractive one to many people. A strong, decisive male breadwinner can protect and be cared for by a gentle, sensitive housewife and mother, and the full spectrum of economic and emotional needs in the family can be met. If both men and women accept their proper roles in this scheme, family life is harmonious and fulfilling, as Dobson explains: 'when (the family) . . . operates as intended, the emotional and physical needs of husbands, wives, and children are met in a beautiful relationship of symbiotic love.'[8] There is a theoretical balance of power in this system, as *Figure 1* indicates. It 'works' because the woman's goodness enables the man's bad behaviour to be reformed, and the woman's wrongness is limited when she puts herself under the leadership and spiritual authority of the man.

Being Right	*Being the Bearer of Righteousness*
Husbands	Wives
Head of the House	Sensitive, Spiritual
'Father knows Best'	'The Angel in the House'
Being Wrong	*Being the Bearer of Wrongness*
Wives	Husbands
Prone to Temptation, Eve	Aggressive, Unspiritual
'Just like a Woman'	'Boys will be Boys'

FIGURE 1[9]

Women as bearers of righteousness are pure, but this makes them unfit to survive in the real world without protection. As soon as women try to make their own decisions, or are faced with temptation, they fall into sin – as readily as did their foremother Eve. There is therefore a reverse side to the idealization of women – the long history of denigrating women, in which Christianity has played all too large a part. Yet despite women's failings, they are given prime responsibility for moulding future generations through the raising of children.

Excuses are made for men's bad behaviour because they are supposed not to be able to help it. Boys 'cannot be expected' to be polite; men 'cannot be expected' to resist their sexual urges when they see an attractive woman. Because masculinity is especially associated with not-caring, aggression and refusal to display emotion, men's failings in these areas are tolerated as normal expressions of maleness. But in the morally imperfect real world, men are supposed to have the qualities to survive. Men's decisions can be right, even though they are 'naturally' bad.

This model has an attractive simplicity. It offers easy answers in an age where relationships between the sexes no longer follow a single accepted pattern. It gives the hope that husbands can become more loving and more Christian if their wives follow the proper course. It offers, too, the promise to relieve women of responsibility over their own lives. It is tempting to suggest that the strong protective Christian male has much in common with the masterful heroes who stride through romantic fiction, and is attractive to women for similar reasons, although I cannot investigate that idea here. But the balance of power is largely theoretical, for the different roles vary in their importance. It is men who make the final decisions, and who have authority and power. Being a symbol of virtue is little consolation for someone who is blamed frequently in daily life. The tension between these two states is clearly illustrated by attitudes towards mothers.

Adrienne Rich describes the 'archetype' of the Mother:

> the source of angelic love and forgiveness in a world increasingly ruthless and impersonal; the feminine, leavening, emotional element in a society ruled by male logic and male claims to 'objective', 'rational' judgement; the symbol and residue of moral values and tenderness in a world of wars, brutal competition, and contempt for human weakness.[10]

Yet day by day, mothers are blamed for all the imperfections in their children's character and behaviour. Posy Simmonds picks up this

contrast between the symbolic value and real experience of motherhood in 'A Mother's Plea'. Christians reproduce the symbol when the Virgin Mary is held up as the perfect representative of womanhood, or when 'The Family', and women's role within it, are idealized with little regard to the ambiguity of women's experience in the home.

Family life is important, and a proper area of concern for Christians, but 'The Family' cannot be held up as a bastion against the immoral forces of a secular age. For real families are often areas of destructive conflict, strained relationships, and even physical and sexual abuse. Sometimes it is those who have suffered from negative experiences of this kind who are the most passionate supporters of 'The Family'. We may know how imperfect relationships are, yet yearn for a secure and perfect haven – and mothers who live up to the ideal.

That yearning is evident in the writings of someone like Goldberg, who claims to write scientifically and impartially as he seeks to prove that male dominance is 'inevitable': 'Few women have been ruined by men,' he states, with an astonishing disregard for the history of women's oppression, but 'many men . . . have been destroyed by women who did not understand, or did not care to understand, male fragility.' He asserts that men in every society 'look to women for gentleness, kindness, and love, for refuge from a world of pain and force, for safety from their own excesses'.[11] Women have the responsibility for creating and providing this refuge in the home. There is a parallel here with Gunn's remark about men being babies who need attentive nuturing from their wives.

As with the description of roles within the family, this picture is one of incomplete human beings, who can only function when put together with the other sex: 'Each has what the other has not; each completes the other. They are in nothing alike, and the happiness and perfection of both depends on each asking and receiving what the other only can give.'[12] This leaves single people at something of a disadvantage! But qualities are not divided between men and women in this way; we are all a mixture of the characteristics stereotyped as masculine or feminine. We are unique individuals, made in the image of God, whose richness and infinite variety we reflect. We need each other for fellowship, and not because a man or woman alone always lacks particular qualities.

It is simply not accurate to describe women, as Brand does, as soft-shelled sensitive creatures who need the protection of men. This makes very little sense for most women in the world, who work long hours, often supporting their families alone, and need great physical and mental strength to do so. The idealization of the feminine as the embodiment of virtue bears little relation to women's everyday lives, and has a particular historical background which is ignored when Christians promote it as God's pattern. The idealized picture of femininity we have today owes much to the historical circumstances surrounding the emergence of capitalism and industrialization. Although it is not possible to discuss it in detail here, it is important to acknowledge this context.

According to Hamilton,[13] the early Protestants had a positive view of women as worthy helpmates for their husbands, which contrasted with the Catholic tradition's more ambivalent view of women and married life. Whilst Protestants believed that women should submit to the spiritual authority of their husbands, their main image of women was as modest, hardworking, loyal and godly wives, who played a full part in the economic life of their society. But society was to change with the emergence of capitalism and industrialization. Protestant teachings on women and the family had been patterned on the household as an economically productive centre, but the home was beginning to change its character. It was becoming a place for private emotions, children, and women; a haven, offering refreshment and escape from the harsh competitiveness of the commercial and public world. This image persists today.

The Protestant emphasis on women's calling within the home was never intended to exclude them from productive labour, or to give them a unique spiritual role in the family. The Protestant intention, says Hamilton, was that the home should be 'a moral and industrious place. . . . Instead, stripped of its productive functions, the home became a spiritual retreat, in need of protection from an, at best, amoral world.'[14] Their identification with the home furthered an identification of women with spirituality and morality, over against the secular masculine sphere of work and scientific rationality. Women came to be seen as less 'fallen' than men. Yet Protestants had not believed that women were naturally saintly in this way. They knew that virtuous behaviour was a continuous struggle for everyone. Few women could come near to the idealized Victorian picture of the 'Angel of the House'. Only the affluent, white, middle-class woman had a chance, and even she could fail.

Some Christians today reproduce the idea that society needs women to preserve the values of morality and tenderness. They argue that because women have opted out of their responsibility to nurture men and preserve moral values, violence and disorder are increasing and family life is breaking down. Brand writes that when women fought for their rights, and began to do well the jobs formerly done by men, they usurped male authority: 'Confused and threatened, many men abdicated all responsibility in their homes, and in society as a whole. They were emasculated.'[15] But this view is too simplistic. It may be convenient to blame social disorders, divorce and family strife on feminism, but men were opting out of their family responsibilities before the most recent feminist movement emerged, whilst many women *were* at home.

This is a very important point, given that so many Christians blame feminism for breaking up families. Barbara Ehrenreich shows how men came to reject the 'breadwinner ethic' in the United States during the 1950s.[16] There were strong pressures to convince men that the breadwinner role was the proper state for the adult male, but men became discontented with their responsibility for wives who stayed at home and devoted themselves to pleasing their husbands. These women were seen as emasculating men, not by taking over their jobs and authority but through their dependence. Men began to rebel against marriage and the family, and to want fun, irresponsibility and escape from the bondage of breadwinning. Women were not contented either, discovering that however hard they tried to find fulfilment in their homes, they were left dissatisfied. Betty Friedan articulated this 'problem that had no name' in *The Feminine Mystique* in 1963,[17] and this acted as a catalyst for the second wave of feminism which is still with us. (The first wave is usually identified as the period 1860 to 1920.) Clearly feminism does have an effect on how women see their roles, but many other factors contribute to changes in our society.

In theory it may appear desirable for a woman to create a haven at home, where a man can recuperate from the harsh struggle of earning a living. As we have seen, many wives wish to provide their husbands with this service, and some jobs would be very difficult to do without it. The cry is often heard from women in professional careers that what they need is a 'wife'. But we do need to recognize that it costs a woman to absorb her husband's frustration, without any outlet for her own; that being a housewife is acutely frustrating if women have other ambitions. It is costly for women because they do not have special qualities which enable them to give continually, to follow what Brand calls woman's 'prime calling', that 'twenty-four hours a day task of giving herself to her world'.[18]

Despite the ease with which some Christians perpetuate the stereotype of women as 'naturally' more caring and sensitive than men, little firm evidence has been found for it in the long history of research into sex differences.[19] Real human beings rarely fit the stereotypes, for we are all a mixture of characteristics. Differences commonly assumed to hold true often do so only on average, or under certain circumstances. For example, whilst on average men are stronger than women, there are many women who are stronger than many men, and in some cultures it is women who are the main burden-carriers. Moreover, the difference in physical strength evens out with age. And whilst men appear to be more aggressive than women, this may be because they show particular forms of aggressive behaviour. Under some circumstances – protecting or using violence towards children, for example – women can be highly aggressive; or their aggression can emerge in other ways, such as verbal abuse.

Similarly, women may appear to be more emotional than men, but this may be because they are allowed to show their emotions more publicly than men in our society. Clearly many men *are* sensitive to the needs of others, otherwise there would be no men in caring jobs. I was interested to hear from one group of male ordinands that they regarded women as more caring and spiritual than men, despite the fact that these were essential qualities for themselves as priests.

The idea that women are 'naturally' nurturant is also open to question. Certainly women have a different reproductive system from men, so that it is they who go through pregnancy and birth, and suckle babies. There are also hormonal changes in women's bodies which can influence their behaviour towards new babies. Hormonal and physiological processes do have an effect, but different women have very different responses. A new mother may be overwhelmed by love for her baby, or may take some time to form a bond, or may wish to give the baby away for adoption. A similar range of responses can be found in fathers, who have not gone through pregnancy and childbirth. Clearly even if there is such a thing as a maternal instinct, it is not found universally, since the neglect and abuse of children by mothers is all too common. And even if it is possible to describe a particular type of sensitive, nurturant behaviour that is found in most women but in very few men (and that is debatable), this does not get us very far.

It might be that the behaviour which women exhibit arises out of the circumstances of their lives, and that men would behave in the same way in the same situation. There are influences on the sexes from the moment of birth which direct them in particular patterns of behaviour. It is probably not possible to separate out what is caused by 'nature' and what by 'nurture', but perhaps it is not necessary either. The most that recent researchers seem willing to say is that there are propensities towards types of behaviour which are sex-linked, but that we have a great deal of choice over what we make of them. For it is far from clear what response even a firmly established 'natural' sex difference should demand from us.

Some Christians believe that once we can discover what is 'natural' for men or women, we shall know what God intends them to do. But men's being 'naturally' dominant, as Richards points out, might be a very good reason for imposing special restrictions to keep their nature under control. Or if women do specialize in certain nurturing skills, it might be in the interests of society for these to be used as widely as possible rather than only for a woman's own family. In any case, whether men and women are 'born the same, or slightly different, or very different, we have the choice . . . of trying to make them more different, or less different, or of keeping the differences more or less the same.'[20]

It is a considerable leap to move from assertions about mothers' behaviour with their own children, to laying down restricted roles for women as a whole. Whilst in some circumstances, it is appropriate to lay down rules which mean a minority must suffer, it is hard to see how this applies to different groups of women. It does no good if women who dislike children, or who are not especially sensitive to the needs of others, are required to be stay-at-home mothers or enter the caring professions. It is much better that such work should be done by those best suited for it, male or female.

We need to question the view of God which underlies the desire of some Christians to have a simple, clear-cut set of rules to follow. God here tends to be seen as an authoritarian figure who tells us what to do, and punishes us – directly, or through the natural consequences of our actions – if we do not obey the rules. Although life seems easier if we can divide everything into good and bad and know exactly what to do in each situation, God's justice and love are much greater, and our world much more complex, than this limited conception allows. We have to work and pray hard to discover God's will in our present situation, and this is one way we grow to Christian maturity.

There are serious consequences when such virtues as sensitivity, gentleness and caring are linked with women and the domestic sphere, for they can then be dispensed with by men and in the 'masculine' public world. Leghorn and Parker express themselves strongly on this point, and there is some truth in what they say:

> Today's world is being run predominantly by men who are totally immersed in male culture and values and who have grown up with a profound sense of male entitlement. For any one group of people to live their lives with the conviction of their natural right to women's subservience and of their own isolation from the sphere of nurturance, sensitivity, and daily maintenance of life work, is appalling. If the world seems to be on a suicidal course, it is because it is being run by people socialized into patriarchal values – insecure, irrational, aggressive, competitive, self-serving, and acquisitive people.[21]

This viewpoint is a challenging one for Christians, many of whom have blamed women's departure from their traditional roles as the cause of the world's 'suicidal course'. But Leghorn and Parker suggest that the problems stem from men pursuing too hard the traditional attributes of masculinity, and these are seldom criticized by Christians.

However, categorizing all men as evil is as unhelpful as idealizing women. Both sexes are a complicated mixture of good and evil, insensitivity and caring. Individuals do vary on these points, but not according to their sex. Men have capabilities for caring, but often neglect that side of themselves because they have learned that it is unmasculine, and relatively few men are in caring jobs which require skills of sensitivity and tenderness from them. This is perhaps beginning to change, as it becomes permissible for fathers to be more involved with their children.

Where women are idealized they cannot be seen accurately, as mere human beings caught up in the mess of life. Women are people who make mistakes and must struggle to be good, whose acts have complex, ambiguous consequences. They are not saints. There is no fundamental difference of 'nature' between the sexes which allows us to ascribe a permanent nurturing role to women. The idealization of the feminine which suggests that women do have special attributes prevents their real frustrations being heard. Yet women have learned that caring is an important part of the feminine role. A woman must be loving if she is to be seen as a 'good woman', and this is the theme of the next chapter.

· *Chapter 3* ·

The beautiful task of serving

The whole of Scripture witnesses with one accord that to man is confided the heavy task of ruling, to women the beautiful task of serving.[1]

The servitude of women, or servant groups, or slaves, has been justified in the name of 'Christian service.' . . . But we should remember that Jesus called males, especially his male disciples, to servanthood. He did not recommend this to people who were already slaves.[2]

Feminism is often labelled as a selfish movement which wishes women to concentrate on their own fulfilment at the cost of caring relationships with others, primarily men or children. The need for women's self-fulfilment needs to be stressed, but increasingly feminists are emphasizing the importance of women's relationships with others. They have pointed both to the lessons to be learnt from women's experience of service, and to the problems which arise from the particular way in which service is related to femininity.

Many feminists suggest that women have qualities of understanding and sensitivity which are needed in the world as a whole. Some find themselves in agreement with the writers described earlier who believe these qualities are 'natural' to the feminine sex, with men being aggressive and almost beyond redemption if they cannot learn 'feminine' values:

Most men's need to prove their masculinity has left them and their culture arrested at an adolescent stage of human development . . .

For men to grow up, they must learn female-value-based behavior (*sic*), which is not simply the performing of jobs hitherto considered female or the expression of emotions. . . Men must put a genuine concern for the needs of others, and a concept of power that is based on co-operation and creativity rather than control, before their egos, competiveness, vanity and need to prove themselves.[3]

Leghorn and Parker appear to fit one feminist stereotype, since they seem to view men with some contempt. Yet this is a common viewpoint in female culture, by no means confined to feminists. It actually underlies some of the Christian writing on relationships between the sexes. In fact many feminists believe more strongly in the possibility of changing men's behaviour than anti-feminists do. Their aim is to 'overthrow the master as a master, in order to reclaim him as a friend'.[4] It is, paradoxically, my feminism which makes me anxious to resist categorizing all men as bad. My four-year old daughter often repeats the idea she has picked up from many sources that girls are sweet and nice and boys are horrible. I regularly point out that some boys are nice, and some girls are nasty, but feel I am a lone voice! Labelling virtues such as concern and co-operation as 'female-value-based' perpetuates sex stereotyping, and is unhelpful.

Although women are not biologically programmed to be caring and selfless, most people seem to accept that this is the ideal to which good women should aspire. In theory, virtue for either sex consists of a selfless concern for others, but it is not a feature of masculinity in the way it is for femininity. Women internalize an ethic of caring in a way men do not. Whether they are doing paid or unpaid work, in the home or outside it, their role is characterized by service. They are expected to care for others, lovingly and with little or no reward. According to Graham, '"Caring" becomes the category through which one sex is differentiated from the other. Caring is "given" to women: it becomes the defining characteristic of their self-identity and their life's work. At the same time . . . not-caring becomes a defining characteristic of manhood.'[5] The woman who says 'no' when confronted with the needs of others is not simply being a selfish person, she is not being a good *woman*. A man who is insensitive and uncaring is following the masculine stereotype; a selfish person, but a normal, and therefore a good, *man*.

The need to serve, as Miller says, 'is not *central* to a man's self-image . . . Once he has become a man, *by other standards*, he may *choose* to serve others.'[6] Thus some men choose lives of self-sacrifice, such as becoming priests or entering monastic orders. But they are unlikely to be condemned if they do not serve in this way. Christians sometimes suggest that men's role in the family is a sacrificial, serving one: 'Loving, sacrificial authority is the uniquely Christian contribution to the understanding of how we are meant to see the father in the family.'[7] Smith speaks of the heavy responsibility men bear for what goes on in their homes: 'We are to carry out this responsibility as servants, there to serve our wives and to provide a framework in which they can grow and develop.'[8]

But there is a crucial difference between this and the kind of service women are to offer, for men are serving from a position of strength. They have sacrificial *authority*, serve as *leaders*. They cannot negate themselves completely and remain authoritative, neither do they forgo status or reward. Husbands must be prepared to make sacrifices, giving up some of their time and energy for their children and the marriage relationship. However serving their wives in this way is not the whole of their lives, as marriage is for women. Generally speaking, men's service does not lead to their being exploited in the way that women often are. This is one reason why it is odd to find Christians insisting that men have a far harder role to play: 'Most women at all times have not found submission easy (. . . however, we should remember that Paul's exhortations to men are infinitely more awe-inspiring and demanding).'[9] The service men are expected to give in this context is demanding, but it affirms them rather than draining away their sense of worth.

The association of femininity with caring gives rise to two difficulties. First, because women's roles are characterized by caring, women themselves are seen as virtuous. Yet often their service arises not from choice but from their feminine conditioning and subordinate position. Miller explains that dominant groups define the acceptable roles for subordinate groups, which tend to involve providing services that the dominant groups does not wish to perform for itself. Certain qualities are attributed to and encouraged in the 'inferior' group, which fit them for these tasks. Because it is the dominant group who have the greatest influence on culture, their perceptions become the norm, and subordinates often internalize the view of themselves as weak, lacking initiative and fulfilled in their serving role. This analysis is applicable to both women and minority ethnic groups.[10]

Because various factors make it difficult for women not to serve others, it is hard to tell whether individual women are serving through choice or because they cannot avoid it. It is simpler to assume that women freely make the good choice because they are 'naturally nice'. Many women would insist that they serve out of the kindness of their hearts, from free choice and not conditioning. But that is the essence of the problem. Because of the expectation that women will serve, their service is taken for granted, and it is not possible even for them to tell whether they are doing it for love or because they have no choice. This prevents women from offering their wholehearted service for the sake of the Kingdom of God.

Second, if women are seen as virtuous by nature, it can be assumed that sacrifice comes easily to them. Men, as 'normal' human beings, cannot live their lives through and for others unless they are great saints. Women are supposed to do this without much difficulty. But women *are* normal human beings, and being human, suffer from constantly denying their own needs for the sake of others.

Miller explores the psychological background to women's serving. She points out that serving others is a basic principle around which women's lives are organized. Girls are taught that their main goal in life is to serve others – first men, and later children. As a girl, I learned that the way to a man's heart was through doing his washing. I recall visiting my student brother and doing his washing for him *by hand*, including heavy pairs of jeans. One woman told me that she was at a college with separate residences for men and women, but only the women's hall had laundry facilities. Women who took on this chore for men were not simply demonstrating love, they were being good women, and potentially good wives! Girls today are still encouraged to be sensitive to what they can do for others. Girls' toys are often miniature tools for female service of men and children – dolls, ironing boards and nurses outfits.

It can be difficult for girls who have grown up with the message that their prime role is service within a family, who then do not go on to marry or have children. Women who have made a positive choice for a single life are subject to pressures from other people who want to 'marry them off'. Childless women are told they are being selfish. It is harder still if they want to devote their lives to husband and children but never marry or cannot have babies. Girls are not trained to be independent or to consider a future where they are not wives and mothers. Miller notes that it is important to realize that many women 'truly cannot *tolerate or allow themselves* to feel that their life activities are for themselves'. Instead, they feel compelled to '*translate* their own motivations into a means of serving others'.[11]

A good example of this process is found in discussions about mothers of small children having jobs. Their employment is generally seen as acceptable if they have to earn to support their families. If they have husbands who are earning, many such women will justify their employment by saying that they are better mothers because they have a job. They often point out that they were stressed and irritable being at home with their children all day, but can now give the children high quality attention, though for shorter periods. What many find difficult is to admit that they want a job for their own fulfilment. If they do so, they are labelled selfish. Christians who write about women's employment back up this attitude by encouraging them to have jobs if it is necessary for their service of others, but not solely to contribute to their own fulfilment.

It might be argued that the tendency to translate one's motivations into a means of serving others is a human one, not confined to women. Thus men might justify seeking promotion because the extra income would benefit their families. Tony Walter believes that people in general seek to translate their desires into needs, and calls this the new morality.[12] But there does seem to be a difference between the sexes here, because serving others is so much a part of femininity. The 'moral imperative' for women is to care for others.[13]

When women are in situations where they are physically faced with the needs of others, they have no choice about responding. Clearly, however stressed they feel, they cannot walk out on their responsibilities of caring for others if this means children will go unfed or those in trouble uncomforted. But many women feel they must do the caring *themselves*. They are reluctant to let someone else look after their children or disabled dependants even for short periods, and find reasons why 'only mum will do'. There is much that is positive about women's willingness to care and to put the needs of others first. But it can lead to their exploitation, and denial of women's own needs. This is one reason why nurses and those working with young children are poorly paid. Any protest action harms those who are already vulnerable, and women are accustomed to follow the moral imperative to care and ensure no one is hurt. This ethos pervades caring jobs of this kind, although some men work in them.

An appeal to women's altruism rarely goes unheeded, yet can divert women's energies from tackling bigger issues. I have often been in mixed meetings where women's issues have been discussed, and found the women in the group over-sensitive to whether the men felt excluded or pained. The women turn their attention to making things easier for the men rather than expressing their own concerns. Women are sensitive to others partly because they are conscious of their own need to be understood and taken into account, and this alerts them to similar needs in others. Women may also be afraid of hurting or offending men. Male anger can be frightening for women, because it can sometimes lead to violence and because men have power in society. 'Inferiors' have to understand what their 'superiors' are thinking, for their livelihood depends on pleasing those above them.

On a wider level, women's altruism may be appealed to in order to deny them a legitimate claim. John Selwyn Gummer appeals to women in the Church of England who seek ordination to the priesthood to suffer in silence to avoid hurting others. He suggests that the Church of England 'must wait and trust that out of the self-denial of women, not for the first time, will come the visible unity we seek.'[14] It seems as if women should take care not to cause suffering to others, even if it is for the sake of long-term good. Yet they themselves are expected to suffer and deny themselves for the sake of others.

The expectation is that women's lives should be 'other-directed' in two senses. Firstly, they are to direct their lives *towards* serving other people. In particular this applies to husband and children, but extends to other relatives, employers, the church and so on. Single women often find that they are expected to be able to give their time to their job or church, because they have no other obvious ties. It is difficult for them to claim time for themselves under these circumstances. Giving attention to their own needs is seen as selfish, and that is an accusation most women are anxious to avoid.

Secondly, women's lives are to be directed *by* others: 'her life is oriented toward his in such a way that direction for her life comes through him', says Clark.[15] In practical terms, married women usually find their lives directed by their husband's job and his needs. But many Christians feel that the husband should make further decisions about his wife's life, such as whether she should have employment, and what tasks she should perform in the church. This is said to be men's role of 'headship', to which women should submit willingly. Single women may be urged to find a suitable man to whom they can submit, since for some Christians, all women should have a male 'head'. Some discussion is allowed, but men are to have the final word, even if they choose unwisely:

> If we wish to be changed by (men's) . . . aid into the kind of beauty and radiance we see Christ producing in his bride, we must learn first and foremost to give these men stature in our eyes, to offer them genuine rights to contest our choices. If their vision is restrictive now, we have no better means of expanding it than to give them real responsibility, not snatch the reins from their hands.[16]

This contrasts with the expectations for men. They may be praised for directing their lives toward service of others, but the man who allows his family to dictate his approach to his job will meet with disapproval. The man who turns down promotion because he wishes to spend time with his family, has obviously not 'got what it takes'.

It is difficult for Christian women to resist having their lives directed in these two ways, given female conditioning, and the fact that self-denying service is a central requirement for followers of Christ. The mark of Christians is love for one another; we are to follow Christ who laid down his very life for us. Therefore it might seem that even if women have been conditioned into loving service of others, they should welcome this and not try to escape it.

In 1932, Nygren published a classic study of Christian love, entitled *Agape and Eros*. This identified Christian love with selfless and entirely uncaused giving: 'Christian love has its pattern in the love manifested by God, therefore it too must be spontaneous, uncaused, uncalculating, unlimited, and unconditional.'[17] Although Nygren has been criticized on various counts by many subsequent theologians, he captures a view of Christian love which is prevalent amongst Christians today.

This view seems to be based on the gospel. Before us always we have the example of Christ, who 'of his own free will . . . gave up all he had, and took the nature of a servant . . . He was humble and walked the path of obedience all the way to death – his death on the cross.' For this reason, writes Paul, we are not to 'do anything from selfish ambition' but are to consider others better than ourselves, and look out for one another's interests.[18] In 1 Corinthians 13 he tells us that 'Love does not insist on its own way', but bears and endures all things.[19] Since Christ has made the ultimate sacrifice for us, how can we hold on to any of our own desires? How can we not pour out ourselves in giving to others without limit and without any resentment or complaint?

It then appears that our Christian service of others must follow this pattern; we are to minister to others as servants. We are continually to be merciful without hoping or looking for any return, however unappreciative those we serve are. Because Jesus saw his role on earth as a servant, those who follow him 'must spend themselves in direct personal service to any who call upon them, without calculation and without any safeguards of dignity'.[20]

Alan Richardson discusses what this means for Christian workers, and suggests that they must 'be dutiful and obedient, and must render godly respect and honour to their masters'. For the 'patient bearing of injustice in the sphere of daily work is a sharing of the sufferings of Christ himself'.[21] Richardson declares that:

> When a man turns to Christ . . . his whole life is sanctified, including his life as a worker. What had formerly been done as sheer necessity, or perhaps out of a sense of duty, or even as a means of self-expression and fulfilment, is now done 'unto the Lord', and becomes joyous and free service and the source of deep satisfaction.[22]

For the Christian worker filled with the joy of serving Christ, such things as injustice, drudgery and hardship have lost their power.

There is undoubtedly truth in this thinking, but it suffers because it does not examine the practical implications of serving others. In particular, service and self-fulfilment are opposed in a way which justifies self-negation and exploitation. Christians who try to follow this pattern can find themselves feeling like failures, however hard they struggle. At one conference I attended, a woman described how she wanted to be loving in her home, to copy the Good Samaritan who put other considerations aside in order to serve someone in need. She had four sons and a husband to care for, and felt she did not always respond to their needs but 'passed by on the other side'. She got impatient, or had other things to do. Another woman responded that Christians were not asked to be doormats; but somehow that answer was not satisfactory. The first woman clearly felt that she was failing as a Christian because she was not loving in the right kind of way. The advice that it was all right to say 'no' sometimes seemed too negative.

The Christian tradition does allow us to speak of love of self, and many Christians repeat the idea that we are not to let others walk all over us. They point out that Paul does not say we should *not* look to our own interests, just that we should consider others as well; that if we are to love our neighbours as ourselves, we must love ourselves. Yet whilst these arguments have some validity, they rarely sound convincing. Instead it seems as if we are trying to find excuses for not giving all we could to others. Self-love or setting limits on our service, feel like concessions to human frailty. We feel that if we really were following Christ, we *would* disregard our own needs and never refuse a request, for true saints do not mind being doormats.

Yet the fact remains that this type of service causes problems. It is impossible for most of us, perhaps for any of us, to give to others without some attention to our own needs. We have to have something of ourselves before we can give it away. We also need to consider what service we are giving, to whom, and the effect of it.

For Christian women, any tension is made worse because of the association of femininity and caring described earlier. Most women are in roles where sacrificial service is expected, yet they cannot properly live up to that expectation. Constant demands for their attention can lead to frustration and resentment; and guilt because frustration and resentment are neither Christian nor appropriate to the good woman. A thorough Christian analysis would let us see that the tension arises because of the place of women in our society. Women in general are idealized, expected to care for others, expected not to put forward their own needs. If they fit this model they are good women, but most do not.

Instead of denouncing the artificial model of femininity and the destructive narrowness of the roles assigned to women, Christians are more likely to reinforce them. Christian women who feel frustrated are seen to have failed individually to accept God's requirements. Once they commit their lives to Christ, they will learn to cope with their situation – but not change it. Discussion of God's calling to women in their homes, for example, tends to concentrate on reconciling women to the narrow confines of their domestic role, rather than challenging the system which creates their difficulties. Thus Brand says that her faith is helping her to see housework differently:

> I recognize my calling to rule in my environment. When my home is a mess, it is clearly un-ruled, in rebellion. Housework now becomes a matter of my divine authority exercised in the living room, recreating an atmosphere which declares God's character and rule. . .

> Woman, you are not just a skivvy . . . you are God's Queen, set up by his royal decree from the dawn of time. Now let's try that dusting again. . . [23]

For King, the daily duties most women perform as a matter of course are paralleled with Christ's sacrifice on the cross: 'our calling most likely will be to the mundane job of dinner on time day in and day out. It becomes that great, unselfish sacrifice that enables us to lay down our lives bit by bit and follow Jesus who totally laid down His life for us.'[24] Some writers suggest that women are particularly privileged to be able to serve in this unselfish way. Theirs is the 'beautiful task of serving', while men have the 'heavy task of ruling'. Stott makes a similar point when he says that women's subordinate, ministering role enables them to show Christ-like humility and self-sacrifice: 'Should not the wife even rejoice that she has the privilege of giving a particular demonstration in her attitude to her husband of the beauty of humility which is to characterize all members of God's new society?'[25] The difficulty is that the real frustrations inherent in women's serving roles cannot be voiced without seeming to go against God.

Yet unless these problems are voiced, there is no chance to solve them. The association between femininity and caring means that women's service is taken for granted, and is not thought to cause any difficulties. But an examination of the caring work women do illustrates how harmful it is to apply the Christian ethic of service in an uncritical way.

· Chapter 4 ·

Housewives are human too

For nothing lovelier can be found
In woman, than to study household good
and good works in her husband to promote.[1]

We consider the work of the woman in the house as essentially
feminine, and fail to see that, as work it is exactly like any other
kind of human activity, having the same limitations and the same
possibilities.[2]

As we saw in Chapter One, what women do in the home is not
recognized as hard work – unless a man is being asked to do it! Yet
most women spend many hours a week doing housework, and know
that it takes its toll. Women are brought up to see the service of
husband and children as their prime role, and it is very difficult for
them to avoid taking on the bulk of domestic responsibility, even if
they also have paid employment. The new 'superwoman' appears to
combine home and job successfully, but this has its costs, as Posy
Simmonds shows in a 'A Superwoman's Day'. The virtues and
problems of women's service can be seen very clearly in the home.

The phrase 'I don't work, I'm only a housewife' reflects the general
attitude towards housework in our society. Because housework is not
paid it is not recognized as work, and does not form part of the gross
national product. Yet it can be said to be productive because it
produces workers for industry or commerce: men who are well-fed,
with clean clothes, and whose children are being cared for. It also
contributes to providing future workers through raising children. The
nature of housework as work is concealed by such phrases as 'care in
the community' and 'the family', when both are overwhelmingly
dependent on the unpaid labour of women. In addition to the millions
of mothers in Britain, it is estimated that there are some five million
carers looking after disabled or infirm elderly people, and the great
majority of these carers are women. In practice, the burden of care
falls disproportionately on women with the least resources. It tends to
be the daughters of working-class elderly people who bear the main
burden of informal care in the community. Although women may be

happy to perform these services, the fact that their labour is invisible means that they do not get the support they need to do the job properly.

Yet even when housework is recognized as proper work, it resists easy definition. It involves doing a variety of tasks, or doing the same task in a number of different contexts. A woman sewing on a button at home, for example, may be doing it as a homeworker, for her husband, for a charity toy sale, to repair a uniform for her job or a dress for a party, or for many other reasons. These are the social relations in which work tasks are done, and need to be understood before those tasks can be properly categorized. Work in the home may be exploitative in one setting but creative in another.[3]

Childcare needs to be included as part of housework, but also resists simple definition. Some aspects of childcare are enjoyable and are not experienced as work. Many of the women who write to childcare magazines for pen-friends list looking after their children as one of their 'hobbies'. Similarly, caring for other dependants must be included, but this, too, usually involves periods of enjoyable companionship. Hobbies such as knitting or cooking contribute to household production, but may not be seen as work.

The tasks which are done in the home can be measured to some degree. Yet one of the most draining aspects of housework is the need to be constantly aware of what is required, and there is a constant stream of thoughts running through women's heads from which there is no escape. It does not necessarily create anxiety, yet not being able to switch off leads to stress. It is trivial – 'did I remember to order three pints of milk for tomorrow?' – yet unless these 'trivial' points are remembered by someone, the whole family will suffer. Coote and Campbell capture this in their list of women's unpaid work:

> Women take care of planning meals, shopping, cooking, cleaning, washing, ironing, mending, equipping and ordering the household, clothing and caring for children . . . remember to pay the milkman; they listen, soothe, praise and comfort their menfolk and their children; they anticipate needs, watch for signs of ill-health or distress, remember where things are, keep spare light bulbs, telephone relatives, and pop in to see the old lady round the corner . . .[4]

The saying 'A woman's work is never done,' reflects the extent of women's responsibilities. It is true that most work is 'never done', unless a decision is made to stop or one leaves the workplace. But for those who live on the job, it is much harder to put a stop to work. Those who do paid work from their homes, such as writers or Christian ministers, have this problem. Yet for a woman with domestic responsibilities it is even more difficult to escape the knowledge of work still to be done. She must sit in the unbrushed armchair watching the undusted television, creating washing up as she drinks her coffee, and constantly listening out for children.

Modern conveniences such as washing machines have undoubtedly made some aspects of housework easier. Yet standards have risen along with the introduction of such technology, and the hours spent on housework have not necessarily been reduced. Some women do what amounts to a thorough spring clean every week. Standards do vary enormously, however. In some families everything is ironed, including underwear. In others, only shirt collars – they are the only part that shows! In any case, it is still true that, as Friedan commented in 1963, housework tends to expand to fill the time available to do it.[5] Women with full-time jobs spend less time on it than those with fewer responsibilities. This is one reason why it is difficult to argue that wages should be paid for housework.

Because housework usually involves caring for husband, children or other relatives, it is regarded as essentially an 'expressive' or 'emotional' role, rather than work akin to paid labour. It is true that mothering is essentially a relationship, and does not have to involve doing the routine tasks of childcare. A disabled mother may be able to do few childcare tasks, or a wealthy mother may employ a nanny, but they are still mothers. However, caring for others usually involves a great deal of physical labour, although there is an 'expressive' side to it – giving emotional nurture and guidance. These two aspects can conflict, particularly when children are small. Children see the house as a play space, whilst housework is done to keep things clean. Housework often involves the use of chemicals, machinery and utensils which can be dangerous, and thus it is difficult to do it whilst children are around. It is possible to do as childcare experts suggest – let the children help with their own dusters or washing-up brush. But this is not always convenient or appropriate, and requires more patience than many mothers have.

For some women, the housewife/mother role is regarded as a full-time (but unpaid) job. This view of motherhood as women's most important job is echoed by many Christian writers. Smith asserts that 'God sees the position of housewife and mother as one of the highest and most important functions in the world.'[6] Yet this concentration on only one aspect of women's work in the world is a product of affluence, since in most parts of the world able-bodied adult women cannot be spared from their work to look after small children full time. However, the idea of motherhood as a job is popular. Penelope Leach writes:

> Being a mother is probably the most exhausting job which exists in Western society. Hours on duty and on call add up to twenty-four per day. There are no overtime payments, time off in lieu, money for unsocial hours. No weekend or holiday breaks are provided, and you only get a tea break if you make the tea yourself. The pay is usually atrocious. No union would stand for it.[7]

Leach and others like her seem to take a perverse pride in a schedule that has wrought havoc with the health of many mothers. No union would stand for that kind of job, whether paid or unpaid, because it would recognize the damaging consequences. If the job of caring for children is so important, it deserves to be rewarded and structured much more generously. It is difficult to see how a worker isolated in the kind of job described by Leach could produce work of a high quality whatever the field. Where the job involves creating a balanced, sensitive human relationship, the task seems impossible.

It is the conditions of the *job* outlined by Leach, rather than the fact of being a mother, which create the problem. Few women live in close-knit communities which can offer the support they need. For most, full-time mothering at home often means being cut off from other adults and outside interests, and leaves mothers especially vulnerable to depression and other psychological disorders. Two 1978 surveys found that a third of mothers with pre-school children were significantly depressed. Meeting other people is known to be important to women, yet motherhood, the central role prescribed for women in our society, is spent largely in isolation.[8]

It is stressful to be constantly on call, whether to small children or other dependants. Yet it may be difficult to have time away where a woman has no friends or relatives to call on, or is living in cramped accommodation. Carers face more problems than do mothers of small children, for whilst most children become increasingly independent, a disabled person requires care for the rest of their life. Where the disability is pronounced, there is a need for 24-hour-a-day care, which can last for many years. There are fewer options open to carers taking

37

a break. Unlike children, adult dependants are not easily amused whilst carers chat. Nor is it simple to take an elderly or disabled person out of the home. There are intense physical strains involved in lifting and managing the weight of another adult, and in any case, our society does not easily accept people with physical or mental handicap in its midst.

Although I have focused mainly on the negative aspects of women's role in the home, I am not denying its positive value, and the fact that many women take it on quite happily. Caring for others can be rewarding, and some women find being a housewife very fulfilling. Many women enjoy particular tasks, especially if they have the time to do them properly: ironing, cooking, tidying, sewing and so on. There can be a sense of being one's own boss, although in fact the choices available to most women are limited in scope. The housewife's days are structured by the continuous cycle of family needs, and she is also governed by the type of job her husband has and the hours he works. A husband's job also influences where they can live and what they can afford.

Women often find satisfaction in fulfilling other people's needs and seeing others thrive under their care. If all goes well, watching a baby grow into a child and on into adulthood brings a great feeling of achievement. Restoring order and cleanliness to an untidy house can also be satisfying. There is a sense of worth to be gained from bearing the main responsibility for the home. Society might regard this as low-status work, but it does give some power and control. This is one reason why women do not always want men doing more in the home. They take pride in successfully combining domestic and other work, and in being able to cope with many competing demands.

For many women, the pleasures of childbearing more than adequately repay them for any stresses involved. Many mothers enjoy their children's dependence on them, and enjoy being essential to babies. Being involved in children's development calls for intelligence, emotional resources and adaptability to change, and women often find this challenging. Motherhood needs to be recognized as a positive, maturing experience. The danger comes where it is seen as the *only* achievement or maturing experience possible for women.

A major difficulty is that motherhood, and to a lesser extent caring and housework, are discussed in extreme terms. They are either idealized or denigrated in a way which bears little relation to the ambiguous ways in which they are experienced. Childcare magazines sometimes feature letters which suggest that women who complain about negative features of motherhood should never have had children in the first place. But motherhood, like other relationships, has both good and bad sides, and the only way to improve it is by discussing it realistically. Such discussions are blocked if every murmur of complaint is met by the suggestion that only a bad mother would make it.

Carers may feel that they have to cope, since the only alternative is for their dependant to be taken into residential care, and this can prevent them voicing complaints. Few carers object to being responsible for the care of their dependants, but most find the conditions under which they are expected to do it very difficult. There is some State help for carers, in the form of day care centres, home help and nursing care in the home, but this is not always appropriate to the needs of individual families, and women seem to receive less support than men, since they are assumed to be able to cope. In one 1982 study of 172 carers, 75 per cent of sons and 68 per cent of husbands got a home help service or informal support from neighbours. Only 4 per cent of mothers, 20 per cent of wives and 24 per cent of daughters received this.[9]

The fact that women experience dissatisfaction in the home is rarely treated seriously. Some argue that even if the role of the housewife is dull and frustrating, it is no worse than most other jobs. The difference is that it is possible to take a break from other frustrating jobs. Moreover, any stress on housewives will be taken out on those for whom they care, and at its extreme this can lead to abuse of children or other dependants. Others suggest that it is only a few middle-class women who resent sacrificing their careers to look after their children. But research in this area has shown that women of all backgrounds can find being a housewife frustrating much of the time.[10] The problems experienced by women in the home are shown by the frightening numbers who take tranquillizers. Depression in women is likely to be treated with tranquillizers, although perhaps less often than formerly, given recent public attention to the problems of addiction to these drugs.

The important point is once again that women are viewed as essentially different from men. Their problems are peculiarly feminine ones, and therefore not treated as they would be in men. Boredom or depression in housewives is seen as an individual problem, caused by maladjustment in individual women. Yet if the same symptoms appear amongst men, they are treated with much more seriousness. Enlightened thinking sees that any boredom men show in their employment is likely to be caused by the circumstances of the job itself, and steps are often taken to reduce their alienation. Housework is work done under certain conditions which would also result in men being depressed and frustrated. Indeed, where men are isolated in the home through unemployment, their problems receive serious attention. Yet housewives who share much of this experience are not only supposed to be able to cope, but may be held up as models for us all in a world of decreasing employment opportunities.

If the problems experienced by housewives are to be relieved, we must start by evaluating their work as ordinary human labour, rather than as a peculiarly feminine role. Doing this makes women's double shift of housework and employment more visible. Women value employment because it gives them a break from caring for dependants, contact with other adults, a chance to use skills and an independent income. But jobs for women are often extensions of their servicing work in the home, and carry some of the same problems, as the next chapter shows.

· Chapter 5 ·

Service on the job

A sphere for genuinely feminine work exists wherever sensibility, intuition and adaptability are needed, and where the whole human being needs attention, whether it has to be nursed or educated or helped in any other way, perhaps by understanding it and assisting it to express itself.[1]

The problem with most women is not to make them work harder but to stop them breaking their backs for a pittance.[2]

Women's caring and service in the home are reproduced in particular ways in the labour market. This is not only because women's jobs are service jobs, but because attitudes towards women in the home are mirrored in the labour market. The domestic pattern, in which women service and support men, influences women's employment at all levels. Primarily, women are to serve others without requiring much reward and without complaining about conditions.

Women's employment in the areas of cleaning, laundries and catering is an extension of housework. Because housework is not recognized for the hard labour it is, it may be thought that such jobs are easy ones for women to do. But they are often arduous and unpleasant occupations, taken on because there is no other suitable employment. Black women, who face the twin pressures of sexism and racism when seeking jobs, are therefore over-represented in this type of employment. As Bryan et al. point out, this situation is based on the white stereotype of black people as fit only for menial work. When West Indians were encouraged to come to Britain in the early 1960s, they found themselves expected to 'fill the jobs which the indigenous workforce were no longer willing to do'. This was predominantly service work as night and daytime cleaners, canteen workers, laundry workers and chambermaids.[3]

Domestic service itself was a major source of employment for women in the past, and there are signs that it is increasing again, as the gap between rich and poor in Britain grows wider. Domestic servants can be grossly exploited, and this is particularly the case for many migrant workers. One Filipino woman tells of how she worked from

8 a.m. sometimes until 1 a.m., given only bread, tea and rice for meals. She was seldom allowed out of the house, and was shouted at for making mistakes. Her employer even wanted her to sleep in the garage.[4] If there is a good relationship with an employer, however, and good conditions, working for another person in their home can be a positive experience. The live-in or daily help may be regarded as one of the family.

Cleaning under contract, in offices, shops or factories, presents a different set of problems. The hours may fit with childcare, but these are often unsocial hours, and may involve travel to non-residential areas at those times. As with many other jobs women do, the work is usually part time, and workers have few rights for holidays and sick leave. Cleaning involves the use of dangerous chemicals as well as manipulating machinery. It can be very unpleasant – cleaning public toilets, for example. The financial rewards are poor, and there are few other satisfactions. As with housework, those for whom the service is performed are unlikely to notice unless it is not done. And people are likely to object if cleaning creates any disruption of their work routines. Cleaning is essential work, but it is meant to be invisible, never impinging on the consciousness of those for whom it is done.

Other areas of employment in which women predominate are associated with their nurturing role in the home. Thus they teach or care for small children, nurse, or service men's work as secretaries and typists. Secretarial work often involves servicing a male boss as a kind of 'office wife', in addition to using genuine secretarial skills. The secretary may be expected to do his shopping, make him cups of tea, and remind him of his family's birthdays as well as his business appointments.

This may seem like an imposition, but it can make a welcome change from routine typing. It can also give a feeling of power, as one secretary admitted: 'If you really take someone on, you can end up running his life – from the dentist appointments to the flowers to the wife . . . which can be quite an ego trip'.[5] Unlike a real wife however, secretaries cannot answer back, since they might then lose their jobs. The author of the following sentence from *High Powered Typewriting Drills*, quoted in the *Guardian*'s Naked Ape column some years ago, clearly had in mind the essentially supportive role a secretary ought to have: 'The true role of women in society is to exhort and inspire man to act . . . and suggest with quiet confidence in order to give him courage and wisdom to meet the trials of life.'

Like cleaners, secretaries may find themselves treated as if they did not exist. This happens at meetings, for example, where the secretary is not introduced and makes no contribution. Being unobtrusive in this way is part of what women are paid for, to provide privacy, comfort and confidentiality for men. Secretaries may also be patronized. They may be known by their first name, whilst their boss retains his formal title. Managers may jokingly say that their 'girl' does all the real work, or is the real boss in the office, but it may be quite true. However, her wages will not reflect it, nor is she likely to be given any formal responsibility or prospect of promotion.

The relationship between boss and secretary is based on a male/superior female/subordinate model in which women service men's needs, as this secretary makes clear:

> My new boss's attitude is chauvinist, and mine is subservient. It's a power-game – a master–slave complex. . . .It could be degrading, but all the secretaries laugh about it when we're on our own; and though my boss treats me in this way when he's with someone, when we're alone in the office it's rather like a marriage – he's very dependent on me, and we've learned to tolerate each other pretty well.

This can cause problems where one or both parties do not fit this model. Women managers may find it difficult to negotiate a proper relationship with their secretaries, and some secretaries do not want to work for a female boss. The relationship between women in employment cannot be disguised as a 'marriage', nor is the same kind of power-game involved. Women bosses may nonetheless treat their secretaries harshly and be unsympathetic to complaints. But problems should fade as women gain more experience of working for one another, and establish a new model for the relationship.

It is not only secretaries who play the servicing role in relation to men. It is satisfying to offer attention and care to others, as Rowbotham explains:

> Female conditioning into self-denying service means that women even with relatively high earnings drop into looking after men . . not because women are a peculiar breed of mugs, but because by doing these tasks (errands, washing shirts) which are expected of them, women at work are subtly flattered that their sex is recognised. This makes them feel that they are not quite on the cash-nexus, that they matter to their employer in the same way that they matter to the men in their personal lives.[6]

This can create a tension for women who wish to show affection for those with whom they work. If they do things for men, it is interpreted in the context of a stereotyped feminine/masculine relationship, rather than accepted as a gesture between equals. When I worked as an industrial chaplain, I tried to leave it to one of my male colleagues to make coffee during meetings because I did not want to take on that feminine service role in relation to them. Several other women in similar situations have told me they had the same approach. Yet when I had a baby, and the chaplains met in my house, I welcomed the chance to serve their coffee, for I could do so quite naturally as the host for the meeting.

Women are also found 'serving' the public, working in such areas as retail, banks, as clerks and as hairdressers. Girls and women often enter such jobs because they involve working with people. There are also theoretical opportunities for promotion or setting up in business on one's own, although women are more likely to find themselves stuck at a low level. There can be satisfaction in such jobs, but shop assistants and hairdressers are poorly paid, and the jobs are tiring because they are on their feet most of the day.

One of the difficulties in service jobs of this kind is that they demand a smiling face and positive attitude. They are what Hubbard calls 'semi-nurturing' professions, for 'each requires above all else the skill to adjust one's needs to those of others, to submerge, subdue, efface one's self.'[7] When people go into a bank or a shop, they wish to be treated as individuals and have their requirements dealt with quickly. Yet it is hard to maintain this attitude for seven or eight hours a day, dealing with a continuous stream of people, some of whom may be difficult or even abusive. Stereotyping of women adds to this, by being especially critical of women who 'gossip' on the job, and of women who contravene the proper feminine role by being unsmiling or unhelpful.

One of the most 'feminine' occupations is that of nursing. The nurse epitomizes the ideal of the good woman. As Florence Nightingale wrote in 1881:

'To be a good nurse one must be a good woman . . . What makes a good woman is the better or higher or holier nature: quietness — gentleness — patience — endurance — forbearance, forbearance with patients, her fellow workers, her superiors, her equals'.[8]

People still make this identification, despite the fact that some nurses are men, and female nurses do not necessarily show these qualities.

Nurses are particularly caught by the restrictions of the service ethic. They are supposed to do their work more out of the goodness of their own hearts than for wages, and are poorly paid given their training, skills, responsibility and often unsocial working hours. Other professions in which people are responsible for matters of life and death are rewarded both in terms of status and pay. Yet because nursing appears to be an extension of women's 'natural' virtue and sacrificial giving, it is thought to need little reward.

Nurses often admit they are 'mugs' to carry on with the job, given the pay and conditions, and increasing numbers are leaving the profession. But it is a potentially satisfying job and enables them to use their skills and training, so many carry on despite the frustration. They are caught because it is very difficult for them to take protest action. If nurses were to go on an all-out strike, their demands would have to be met. But since patients would die or suffer, this is simply not an option for them. There have been days of limited strike or protest action by nurses, but since they take care that suffering is avoided as far as possible, the action loses its impact.

The assumption that women work for love rather than for reward, or that they gain reward from the work itself rather than wanting status or pay, is reinforced by their involvement in voluntary work. This presents a problem with which Christians have been slow to grapple. Christian women are frequently advised of the many opportunities for voluntary work they might undertake if they do not need employment for the money. Yet if some people will do a job without asking for wages, it takes away the bargaining power of those who do need a proper wage for similar work. It is not, of course, only women who do voluntary work, yet they form the majority of those involved in it, and this has influenced the way it is perceived.

Around a quarter of employed women work in manufacturing industries, mainly food and drink manufacture, clothing and footwear, textiles and electrical engineering.[9] They seem willing to do tedious, repetitive, soul — and health — destroying work for low wages, and this makes them useful to employers. There are many reasons for this situation, which cannot be discussed properly here.[10] Most women seem to accept whatever job they can get, particularly if this fits in with their domestic responsibilities. There are small numbers of women doing non-traditional jobs, working in manual trades or in professional, managerial and scientific jobs. Yet even here, they face certain expectations based on the fact that they are women. There are also male secretaries, nurses and so on, who face some of the problems associated with service of others. Moreover, the fact that they are doing 'women's work' can create difficulties for men, because they are then seen as unmasculine.

The majority of men probably understand their work as service in a different sense, which it is worth noting here. They may perceive their masculine breadwinning role as sacrificial service undertaken for wife and children. There is, says Willis, 'an element of self-sacrifice in men's attitude to work – slow spending of the self through the daily cycle of effort, comfort, food, sleep, effort'. Because this is for the home, 'there is dignity and meaning, even in sacrifice'.[11] There is also a type of middle-class masculine service which Tolson describes as a 'notion of "privilege", tempered by "duty" and "service", supposedly inherent in the masculine character. A man is born to lead, but also, paradoxically, to serve those he leads.'[12]

But this type of service is not subject to the constraints of the Christian ethic in the same way that women's work is. That is, men are not expected to work without complaint, without reward, and without regarding their own interests. It can be costly, but rather than eroding a man's sense of identity it often represents a bargaining counter. After an eight-hour shift he has the right to the evening in the pub; after a week of top-level decision making, he needs his Saturday morning on the golf course. It is much harder for women to take time off in this way, especially if they are mothers. Their evenings out often have to be negotiated; they are not a right.

One area of men's work where they are more subject to an ethic of service is in the armed forces. They are encouraged to believe they are defending their country, their women and children, and that to sacrifice their lives for this purpose is glorious. Christian values are evoked either explicitly or implicitly, in the manner of Cecil Spring-Rice's well-known hymn:

> I vow to thee my country . . . the service of my love:
> The love that asks no questions, the love stands the test,
> That lays upon the altar the dearest and the best,
> The love that never falters, the love that pays the price,
> The love that makes undaunted the final sacrifice.

Armed forces are probably a necessity in today's world, but the reality of war and its political machinations are obscured by the language and

culture which surround fighting. Studies of the Falklands war suggest
that the ideology is still strong today, and those who were badly
wounded or died for their country often found the ideology hollow.[13]
As with women's work, the idealization of service prevents the proper
questions being asked.

Within the range of jobs discussed above, women are likely to be
grouped at the bottom. There are still few women in management,
even in industries with a predominantly female workforce. Large
numbers of women teach, but relatively few are heads, even in junior
schools. Even where women do progress in their jobs, they meet with
both conscious and unconscious sexism.[14] For black women, these
aspects of women's work are compounded by the racism inherent in
British society, and they are likely to have the least attractive work.
Asian women are over-represented in the textile and clothing
industry, repetitive assembly work and as homeworkers. West Indian
women tend to be in low-grade professional work and service
industries.[15]

Motherhood has a profound effect on women's employment, for it
restricts the opportunities available to them and influences what is
thought suitable for a woman to do. As one of the key features of
women's employment in recent years has been the growth in the
numbers of married women, and therefore mothers, in the labour
market, increasing numbers of women are affected by this.

Britain has little good daycare provision either for small children or
for children out of school hours. There are thus practical difficulties
for employed mothers, since it is almost always mothers who are
responsible for caring for children. Most get by through a variety of
informal arrangements. Children may be looked after by relatives who
live near by, or by fathers who are available during the woman's
working hours. There are good nurseries and childminders or for the
wealthy, nannies. But too often mothers have to leave their children
in less than satisfactory circumstances, and there is an urgent need for
good daycare facilities and more flexible employment for mothers. In
addition, support is needed for mothers who do not wish to take
employment.

Most Christians suggest that mothers of small children ought to be
at home with them full time, because they not only believe that this is
God's pattern but that it is necessary for the sake of the children. Yet
throughout history, including New Testament times, women have
combined productive work with childrearing responsibilities.

47

Industrialized societies like our own make it difficult for women to do both tasks, but this does not mean that the relatively recent Western ideal of full-time mothering at home embodies God's will for all women. Probably the majority of mothers of small children do not wish for full-time employment, but there is no evidence that children are harmed by their mother's employment, if good alternative care is provided.[16] Children will face some disadvantages because their mothers are in employment, but equally, some suffer through being with their mothers all the time. Families are composed of different individuals, and have very different circumstances. Each family needs to work out the best pattern for them, taking into account the wishes of all involved. Christians will also want to ensure that each family member is enabled to follow their God-given calling, whoever that may be.

There has been much debate about whether mothers ought to take employment. Concentrating on this area, however, prevents recognition of the shared problems encountered by women whether they are at home or in employment. The difficulties which arise from the relation between women, service and the Christian ethic need tackling so that women in all situations may be freed to offer the wholehearted service which can enrich all our lives.

· Chapter 6 ·

Serving without complaint

Lord . . . it matters not at all
That my poor home is ill-arranged and small.
I, not the house, am straightened Lord, 'tis I!
Enlarge my foolish heart that by-and-by
I may look up with such a radiant face
Thou shalt have glory even in this place;
And when I slip or stumble unaware
In carrying water up this awkward stair
Then keep me sweet, and teach me day by day
To tread with patience Thy appointed way.[1]

If . . . you are humiliated, oppressed, kept down by petty intrigue, sheer evil, jealousy, hatred, well then as Christians your task and mine is quite clear . . . we are to die publicly and openly as our Lord did, thus helping our oppressors to see what they are doing to us, for we are not called to stoicism, to heroic indifference to suffering, but we are called to say with Christ, 'God forgive you for what you are doing.'[2]

When women's serving work is interpreted as Christian service, it not only prevents a proper understanding of that work, but misinterprets the meaning of Christian service. It provides spurious theological justification for women's oppression through what I have called the 'service ethic'. This asserts the value of the sacrificial giving of oneself in service, without complaint and without seeking reward. It is problematic not because love and self-sacrifice are wrong, but because these qualities are misunderstood. Moreover, they are not necessarily the appropriate virtues to emphasize for women: 'It is simply *not* Good News to someone trying to break out of the "servant class" to hear that God has called her to be a servant.'[3] Virtues such as love, meekness, obedience and self-denial, which are particularly appropriate for men given their dominance in the world, are taken to heart by women.

The first difficulty with the service ethic is the idea that for service to be properly Christian it must be done without complaint. The worker who is angry about working conditions or frustrated in their job is not being a good Christian, a good person, or a good worker. A good Christian accepts suffering as a share in the suffering of Christ. A good person would not dream of criticizing others. A good worker obeys without question what their employer asks of them. For women, in addition, the archetypal good woman is quiet and self-effacing. A man who is angry and complains is following an accepted masculine pattern. A woman is unfeminine when she does so, and may be labelled strident and aggressive or neurotic and whining. This problem may be worse for West Indian women in white society, because they are stereotyped as aggressive, and thus even further from the ideal of femininity. The need for approval is strong, and may lead to women bottling up any resentment where venting it is a sign of failure to be feminine.

Women may be unwilling to admit to any problem in their lives, since this indicates failure to fulfil the conditions of selfless service. For Christian women, difficulty in the serving role can indicate that they are not in the will of God. King suggests that women who follow Christ are enabled to cope with difficult lives. She writes: 'if God who is the lavish giver of time has called us to follow Jesus, then there will be enough time to do everything He has called us to do', whether we are housewife or missionary.[4] Thus stress and feeling harassed – features which are common amongst mothers and carers – can point to failure in a woman's Christian life rather than a failure in social organization.

Descriptions of how a truly godly woman might organize her home sound wonderful, but present women with an ideal they cannot possibly reach. Brand describes women as 'queens', ruling the environment for God. When 'she comes to the jeans on the floor, she is not a defeated housewife who has to do this every three days and get nowhere, she is queen of her home. She switches on her supply of creativity.' She can decide how to teach her son to tidy up for himself, and she can wash those jeans with serenity and joy.

> When Baby Jane cries from the bedroom, she tunes in to her sensitive antennae to know what Jane wants and needs . . . As she picks her up to feed her, she can not only love her and reassure her, but she can rule Jane's environment too, with a variety of means from a clean nappy to a new game, from a lullaby to a warm bath or a feed.[5]

And if Baby Jane does not respond to this, one speaker at a Mission

England conference said that God gives women special abilities to cope with the yelling child.

Yet this implies that the majority of Christian mothers, whose children do yell or are unresponsive to attempts to soothe them, are failing in their Christian lives. Being made to feel failures does not automatically spur people, and especially women, on to trying harder. It leaves them with even fewer resources with which to cope with difficult situations.

Women in general may feel they must show themselves to be fulfilled in their caring role and coping well with it. Human beings do seem to have an enormous capacity to cope with whatever life throws at them, and to find humour, friendship and hope amidst even acute deprivation and oppression. Yet as Graham suggests, many women subscribe to an ideology of 'coping'. It is weakness to need help or make a fuss. Coping successfully means not being seen to do things, denigrating oneself by saying 'Oh, it's nothing really.'[6] Resorting to outside help appears as an admission of failure to cope with something other women manage quite easily. Amongst themselves, women can and do complain about the circumstances of their lives; but they like to be seen as in control nonetheless.

Yet much of women's 'coping' is simply getting by from day to day; often they are not in control of their situation. The mother of a young baby who cries all the time, or the carer whose husband no longer knows who she is, both cope in the sense of continuing to look after their dependants. Met out in the street, they may mention their problems, yet smile and say they are managing. But in the privacy of their homes, they may not know how they can get through another hour. They carry on, because the alternative is to break down and perhaps have child or husband taken away from them. There are many organizations which offer help, and some women are lucky to have friends around them; but the 'marvellous' way in which so many women cope can be a façade behind which they feel themselves to be losing their grip.

The fact that they appear to cope can prevent women getting help. 'Val' describes the first six months of caring for her mother as a nightmare, in which 'My doctor's cheery "You're coping marvellously. You don't need any help, do you?" was intended as a compliment, but it successfully cut me off from all sources of information and support.'[7]

It may only be possible to survive a harsh situation by accepting it fatalistically, and some Christians will see in this the virtue of serving without complaint. It may even be suggested that it is a privilege to suffer, if this is in the service of others. In the face of this, any complaint seems selfish and petty. But as Soelle points out, acceptance of suffering is not necessarily the proper Christian response. The Christian cult of suffering, she says, 'has been shamelessly exploited to justify injustice and oppression', but 'goodness is not mixed with a toleration of injustice'.[8] Christians are often urged to accept and be transformed through suffering, but when this is put forward as the only Christian response, it prevents a proper rebellion against the existence of suffering and what it does to people.

A service ethic which emphasizes refusal to complain, and accepts any personal cost as suffering for Christ's sake, leaves unjust working conditions unchallenged. Unless love for others includes a concern for justice, the ethic of service is used to legitimize oppression and maintain an unjust status quo.

It can be dangerous where people have no legitimate outlet for their feelings of frustration, anger and resentment. If these feelings cannot be directed at their proper cause or discussed openly, they tend to be directed elsewhere, perhaps by blaming inappropriate targets. For example, women who had no choice but to give up careers when they wanted children may be angry not with those who took away their choice, but with women who have been able to combine the two. People may also try to suppress their anger, turning it in upon themselves. As Campbell says, Christians in particular are encouraged to 'bottle it up for God', but this can lead to symptoms of stress, such as physical illness, or 'we can feel resentful and unappreciated, or we can be so depressed that we are incapable of love of self or of others anymore'.[9] These problems are all common ones in women, and also in ministers who similarly are not expected to display resentment.

It is particularly hard for women in the home to admit their anger or frustration. They love those who are the cause of their distress, and when they resent a family member they feel guilt. It is also difficult to express frustration with some of the circumstances of the caring role without seeming to reject both the role and those cared for altogether. Bringing up small children does at least offer rewards as the child becomes more independent and responsive. But a disabled dependant is likely to become progressively less responsive. Although it may be entered into freely and lovingly, the circumstances of caring can kill love, leaving only resignation or a sense of duty. This can lead to feelings of guilt, for the only way out of the situation is the end of the caring relationship. Either the relative has to go into institutional care because the carer can no longer cope, or release comes when the person cared for dies. Wishing for relief from the situation feels like wishing for the death of a loved person, and cannot be indulged.

Feelings of guilt are common amongst women. If the circumstances of their lives make them frustrated and angry, but they regard these feelings as unloving or unchristian, they will feel guilty. This is one reason for the self-deprecation and chronic feelings of inferiority found in many women. A number of feminists have discussed the low self-esteem, lack of confidence and diffuse feelings of guilt, anxiety and insecurity which are common psychological features amongst women in our society. The self-image of West Indian women may be much stronger than that of white women, given their history of having to take responsibility for their families, and combat racist attitudes. On the other hand, any sense of inadequacy may be reinforced for black women living in a society which denigrates them, as Amrit Wilson shows.[10] The question posed by Miller needs attention: if they 'are all so good, why do women feel so bad?'[11]

One answer is that women as a class are 'bearers of wrongness', blamed and denigrated, and this leads to a sense of guilt. They suffer from what Schaef calls 'the Original Sin of Being Born Female', and goodness and right actions are not enough to absolve them of this sin.[12] Women constantly accuse other women of making them feel guilty. Debates over 'working mothers', being married or single, even the way babies are fed, are full of comments about being made to feel in the wrong. Such discussions are often a waste of energy, for the real issue is that women feel they are in the wrong *whatever* choice they make.

Women feel guilt because they can never be good enough, given the circumstances under which they serve and the idealistic definitions of Christian service which are applied to them. They not only feel like failures, but failure further confirms how guilty they are. This can be seen most clearly in women's role as mothers, for motherhood in our society is closely associated with guilt and anxiety.

The idealization of mothers as symbols of love and caring in a harsh world creates problems, since mothers inevitably fail to live up to this high ideal. Indeed, the failure of confidence in being a mother 'is such a familiar syndrome in the West that we hardly comment on it any more,' says Kitzinger, 'anticipating that the new mother will be awkward, unsure of herself, anxious and readily distressed'. Yet as Kitzinger notes, this particular psychological reaction to motherhood is almost unknown in other cultures, where the new mother has much more support.[13] We live in a competitive and technically specialized society, and having and rearing children have become subjects for experts, skills that must be learnt, so as to produce better children than other parents do.

The anxiety mothers are prone to springs partly from the weight of responsibility which rests on a mother who is the sole caretaker of her child. An unforseeable accident or small mistake can have tragic consequences, since small children are highly vulnerable. The feeling may be more acute because of the mother's emotional involvement. Many people in their daily work bear great responsibility over the lives of others, but it is recognized that in order to do such jobs effectively, a certain amount of detachment is needed. A surgeon cannot grieve over every patient he or she is unable to save. A social worker who identified too closely with a client would be unable to do the job properly. Yet mothers are encouraged to devote their lives to their children, without any time off – and are then blamed for being over-involved.

Mothers are also often blamed for any behavioural or physical difficulties in a child. Whatever they do seems to be wrong, as Posy Simmonds shows in 'Momma's Fault!'. This may even include blaming the mother's activities or emotional state in pregnancy: 'If the pregnant woman is emotionally disturbed (or perhaps even harbors negative attitudes), the foetus is adversely affected . . . and a life is launched with impaired developmental potentialities.'[14] Recent developments suggest that the actions of the pregnant woman could lead to her prosecution for child abuse. In 1986 a Californian woman was prosecuted for contributing to her son's death by taking drugs during pregnancy. According to the British Standing Committee on Drug Abuse, 'the logical outcome . . . was that there should be an investigation every time a child was born with some mental or physical defect to see if the mother was at fault'.[15]

Clearly, mothers' behaviour does affect children from the earliest stages, but so do many other factors; fathers, environment and cultural expectations all have an influence. It is dangerous to assume that parents can ever have perfect children. Christians need to insist that universal human sinfulness is taken into account. Moreover,

55

children have their own autonomy, and also influence the way their parents behave. Falsely laying all blame at the door of mothers only serves to increase women's feelings of anxiety and guilt – and makes them worse mothers.

Women may try to rid themselves of their feelings of guilt either by embracing the sufferings self-sacrifice involves, or by trying to justify themselves through their actions. These strategies are not necessarily used consciously, yet their pattern can frequently be traced in women's behaviour.

The story of the Fall suggests that women's pain in childbirth results from the entry of sin into the world. A common theological interpretation of this has been that such sufferings are a *punishment* for sin:

> 'groaning in pain, cramped in travail, humiliated, overburdened, care-worn, and tear-stained' (Vischer) . . . Whence these sorrows . . . this degradation in the woman's life? It is not a small matter that our narrative absolves God's creation of this. Here a primeval offense receives its consequences, which faith recognizes as a punishment inflicted by God.[16]

'Bringing forth children in sorrow'[17] has been interpreted more widely to apply to the raising of children; and women's suffering in motherhood, their acceptance of punishment, has been seen as the means by which they expiate the sin of Eve. By the beginning of the twentieth century, motherhood was discussed largely in terms of suffering and sacrifice. However, maternal and infant mortality rates were high, and this theological interpretation made some sense. In 1915, for example, the maternal death rate was 1 in 250, comparable with the present-day 1 in 7,000.[18] In religious terms, the sufferings of motherhood could be seen as the wages paid to gain heaven, and the mother's sacrifice was evidence of her saintliness. Such an interpretation of God's words to Eve is rare today, although Richardson's comment on Genesis 3 that the 'woman's child-bearing is a sharing of the redemptive burden that must be borne',[19] hints at it. This view of the sufferings of motherhood can have a negative effect on children, who know that their mother regards their care as a sentence she must carry out, or as a cross which she must bear.

There is a tendency to assume that women *should* suffer. The language of punishment used by Bowlby when he writes, 'if you don't do your five years hard labour when the child is young, you do it later',[20] reflects this idea. It may be due partly to a fatalistic acceptance that there is no alternative. But there are also other elements. Older women may feel that because they suffered in their time, younger women must now take their turn. One feature of this may be the 'martyr syndrome'. Some women seem to exaggerate the suffering they have gone through – in labour, with their health, in the conditions under which they have lived – and to delight in complaining to others. Showing how much they have suffered may help them to feel free of guilt, since they have 'paid' for their sins. It also allows them to feel morally superior to those who have had easy lives.

In the past, children's behaviour could be used to judge whether their mother had properly expiated her sins. Thus successful childbearing could confirm a woman's status before God. If, as in Calvinism, good works are a way of proving that salvation has been achieved, the mother who produces 'good' children shows that she is saved. Some Christians give theological support to this idea by translating 1 Timothy 2.15, a notoriously obscure text, as 'women will be saved through childbearing', and interpreting this to mean that motherhood is women's primary calling.

The idea that women are justified through childbearing is also reflected in the popular belief that 'Good mothers don't have bad children.' A mother is judged according to how well her children behave, but this has difficult practical and psychological implications. If children are made responsible for their mothers' standing in the eyes of the community and indeed of God, an intolerable burden is placed on them, for they must succeed in order to justify their mothers' sacrifice. This adds to the difficulties all children have of establishing their own identity in the world and making their own mistakes.

A mother may measure herself against her neighbours, insisting that her methods of childrearing are better than those of others, because this enables her to feel superior. It also wards off anxiety to feel that difficulties in other people's children are due to bad parenting, rather than misfortunes which could happen to anyone whatever they do. It is clear from the histories of childrearing that many different methods have been tried, and each has its own merits and demerits. Whilst mothers can provide a positive environment for children which will help them to develop into mature adults, there will always be stresses within the family or outside which hamper that development. The ideology of motherhood may speak of the possibility of problem-free parenting if the right methods are followed, but children are never perfect:

> Having children is risky. To try to be sure we'll have the 'right' kind . . . is likely to increase the chances that we'll go wrong . . . we have the best chance of successful parenthood if we are prepared to accept our children, whoever they are, and do the best we can to help them accept themselves.[21]

Women need to stress this more realistic assessment of parenting, rather than accepting blame for all the imperfections in their children and in society. 'Working mothers' in particular have been scapegoated as responsible for such things as increases in vandalism and other crimes, despite the lack of evidence. But mothers at home fulfil society's expectation of what makes a good mother, and those with jobs do not. Therefore the latter frequently feel guilty. As Harper and Richards point out, two stereotypes are available to women: 'If you stay at home you are dreary and boring; if you work you are harried and selfish . . . . You can be a dull person or a bad mother'.[22]

Harper and Richards' work is important, because they show that the real issue is not the deprivation of children, but how mothers are to be judged:

> While the idea that 'mother's care is best' is based on the children's needs, the exceptions suggest that it is the mother's own self-image that is threatened more often than the child's welfare. It is, by implication, her guilt, not the child's deprivation, that is the evil to be avoided.[23]

This means that if a mother has to take a job to support her family, it is acceptable for her children to be cared for by other people. It is as if children are not hurt if the need is real. This view is echoed by some Christian writers. Many repeat the idea that working mothers are to blame for the ills of society, without recognizing the negative aspects of full-time mothering at home.

The ideal of serving without complaint is dangerous because it prevents us from recognizing and dealing with guilt, anger, frustration and inability to cope. It causes additional problems when women resort to the inappropriate ways of responding to these negative feelings described above. Yet women are encouraged to carry on serving without being critical of their situation, and few consider the implications for those who are on the receiving end of sacrificial, selfless service. This important issue is the theme of the next chapter.

· Chapter 7 ·

On the receiving end

Somewhere deep inside my head . . . is some glorious image of the
ideal woman . . . She is Ruth and Esther and Jesus and Mary rolled
into one. She always turns the other cheek. She is a vehicle, a
vessel, with no needs or desires of her own. When her husband
beats her, she understands him. When he is sick, she nurses him.
She cooks, keeps house, runs the store, keeps the books, listens to
everyone's problems . . . She is capable of absolutely everything
except self-preservation.[1]

Good Lord, give me a personality . . . I seem only to have been a
service of respondings and no core.[2]

Some Christian writers stress that mothers should not do everything
for their children, since children need to learn to contribute within the
home – King has some useful advice on this point. But women are still
urged to put the needs of husband and children first, and there is little
attention given to the effect this has. From the stories which illustrate
the literature addressed to Christian women, it would appear that if
women submit gracefully to their husbands and concentrate on
putting their menfolk first, those men become mature, authoritative
leaders in their home, and harmony reigns. The hierarchical ordering
of relationships between the sexes may bring harmony of sorts, but it
does not challenge women and men to learn the mature, reciprocal
love for one another which is the Christian pattern.

Men who are constantly on the receiving end of women's
submission and service will find it difficult to learn to serve and submit
to others. Posy Simmonds in 'Sharing' even has George Weber feeling
hard done by because his wife has done all his chores and deprived
him of his chance to feel oppressed. The serious point here is that men
need to appreciate what it is like to cope with domestic
responsibilities, and not to have their wives step in as soon as they
begin to find it difficult. There is little incentive for men to get
involved in an area of work when they know that women will
eventually do it for them. I knew of one woman with four children and
a full-time job who also did all the work in their large garden whilst her

husband relaxed. One year she announced that she could no longer manage the garden, and the rest of the family would have to do it. The months passed, it got into a terrible state, and she found it difficult to live with. But eventually, grumbling, her husband and children tackled the mess. In fact, her husband discovered a talent for gardening which might have remained hidden if she had carried on doing everything herself.

Things do not always work out this smoothly, but it is an important step when women say 'No, you must do that yourself.' It can be difficult not to interfere, but it is essential to stand back to enable others to grow. In the domestic sphere, women who have become too ill to do anything often find their husbands are very quick to learn to run the household and to care for children.

Constantly being a recipient of service, lovingly tended both physically and emotionally, may seem highly desirable, but it does not help personal growth. If all one's behaviour, however outrageous, is met with patience and self-sacrifice, it is difficult to learn that limits have to be set. Someone who is on the receiving end of women's self-sacrifice, may come to ignore her as a person, treating her as if she existed only to serve them. But people should never be taken for granted in this way, and women should try to ensure that their own humanity is recognized.

There are increased pressures on children who are the means to fulfilment for a mother who lives through their achievements. Some Christians, however, encourage women in this indirect way of having an impact on the world. Brand says that women's 'ruling' the home environment has international significance, for 'we may never actually rule nations, but all men who rule in any sphere were originally sons, and were largely shaped by mothers'.[3] This is a rather simplistic statement in any case, but belief in it has caused untold heartache to sons who feel they have to succeed in the world for their mothers' sakes. Whilst the grown man whose mother will not leave him alone is a stock comedy figure, such behaviour can cause great psychological damage.

This attitude towards children reflects the need to be needed. Given that girls learn early on that their fulfilment is to come through serving others, it is not surprising that many women feel like this. It is a further problem created when women sacrifice themselves for others, and can happen in both paid and unpaid caring situations. It becomes dangerous where women try to keep those they care for dependent. A housewife or mother may seek to feel indispensable by making and keeping husband and children dependent on her. Professional carers, too, may seem totally altruistic, giving up their own comforts in order to serve. But they too may need to be needed, and deny that those they care for have any strength or can give anything back. This holds back those cared for from taking responsibility for themselves.

It can be difficult balancing service of others with a proper encouragement of independence, and this tension is apparent in the relationship between mothers and daughters. Eichenbaum and Orbach point out that mothers must prepare their daughters to become givers: encouraging and reinforcing 'a daughter's moves to be caring, to develop her emotional radar, to be responsive . . . to pay attention to others' needs'.[4] But at the same time, mothers must pass on the message that girls are unlikely to have their own emotional needs met as they grow up. Mothers want both to love and care for their daughters protectively, and to teach them that their role is to be givers not takers. In particular, mothers may look to daughters for the emotional contact they are missing in their marriages. Few men are attuned to women's needs in the way that women are sensitive to those of men.

Unfortunately, women may believe that their own needs will be met if they concentrate on others' needs, and that they will be loved *because* they are serving others so much and so well. But love is not generated by such service, even though dependency may be. Men and children may resent that very dependency, and hate the person who is taking care of them.[5]

There is a strong thread in female culture which treats men as children. Despite the subordinate position ascribed to women in society, amongst themselves women often treat men with some contempt. As Arcana points out, mothers tell daughters that men are sources of trouble, and not to be trusted: 'We are taught to consider men brutal, insensitive, emotionally inadequate and highly needful of nurturing and pampering, requiring special handling like babies or convalescents; we are shown how to trick them, demonstrate false affection and/or sexual passion, trap them into giving us money and social security . . .' and even to disguise our bodies, because men appreciate the false image.[6]

Women treat men as children by adopting a protective servicing role which assumes male helplessness and vulnerability. This is quite different from a division of labour within the home because it allows men to escape their proper responsibilities by making excuses for them. One reason for women's infantilizing of men is that this puts them in a position of power, albeit in a limited sphere. A wife can feel superior, because she has special skills and expertise which her husband lacks.

Women are encouraged to treat the male ego as psychologically vulnerable, and to accept that men need to feel superior to women. Men are then completely dependent on women's co-operation, to reassure them that they really are superior and dominant. If women do co-operate, the relationship is built on a lie; if they do not, the man's ego suffers.[7] This is true of relationships in the workplace. Women may be in junior positions, but find they have more experience and knowledge than men who are newly appointed over them. They have to tread carefully to ensure that the job is done properly but allow their male superiors to take the credit.

Within marriage, a similar problem arises, as Gornick and Moran point out:

> There are few trauma greater than . . . the wife's discovery of her husband's dependencies . . . of her own gut-superiority in a thousand hidden crannies of the relationship; than the realization that in many situations his judgement is no better than hers; that he does not really know more than she; that he is not the calm, rational, nonemotional dealer in facts and relevant arguments . . . Equally . . . serious is her recognition that she is not really the weaker vessel, that she is often called upon to be the strong one in the relationship. These trauma are the more harrowing because they are interpreted as individual, unique, secret . . . not even . . . to be admitted to oneself.[8]

The man too will suffer if he realizes he is not really dominant, for this leaves him acutely vulnerable to the woman who knows him. Most women are reluctant to hurt men by exposing the lie, and Christian women are often encouraged to protect men's ego in this way. Advice on how to 'manage' men is prevalent in both Christian and non-Christian literature for women. Although male headship is said to be commanded by God, many men have no leadership abilities, or are less intelligent and capable than the women around them. Nonetheless, wives are instructed to submit to their husbands: 'God's order for the family applies regardless of the intelligence or achievements of either partner. The husband is the spiritual head, not necessarily the family Mastermind.'[9] Barth states that man's role is to stimulate, lead and inspire. Woman must grant him this place gladly, even if he acts or leads wrongly and this causes her suffering.[10] Although women must not appear superior, they can surreptitiously try to change their husbands' decisions and behaviour. This is, however, a highly manipulative way of conducting a relationship.

Undoubtedly it works in a limited sense, because both sexes can retain belief in their own superiority. Husbands may allow their wives to manage them inside the home because it is clearly men who control wider society. Women gain a sense of power because they see how vulnerable men really are. They can draw prestige from feeling that they are saving someone superior and powerful from making mistakes or having weaknesses exposed. This was one of the positive parts of the job identified by secretaries.

If more honest relationships are to develop between the sexes, women must cease to regard men as incompetent children. Women must, says Rich, 'put down the grown-up male children we have carried in our arms . . . and move on, trusting ourselves and them enough to do so . . . we will have to expect their anger, their cries of 'Don't leave me!', their reprisals'. This means ceasing to treat men as if their 'egos were of eggshell, or as if the preservation of a masculine ego at the expense of an equal relationship were even desirable'. Women must expect men to behave as equals without being thought special. Men may see this as hate, and say that they will 'perish emotionally without our constant care and attention'.[11] But instead of perishing, men can discover their own capabilities for caring, something the world desperately needs.

This course is a hard one for both women and men to follow, but it does offer the hope of mutual interdependence more akin to the Christian ideal. For the Christian principles which govern ordinary human relations still apply within marriage; respect for the other person is essential. If Arcana is right that women regard men as brutal, insensitive and emotionally inadequate, requiring special handling, there is a serious problem. Christians should challenge this stereotyping of men, not adapt their view of marriage to accommodate it.

We have seen that Christian teaching stresses the virtues of humility, service and self-sacrifice, and that women in particular strive to achieve them. But many feminist theologians have pointed out that these virtues are emphasized by *men*, who define the human situation in terms of pride and inability to relate and care for others. Salvation in this case must involve the breaking down of pride, and enable sacrificial service of others. But for women, the main sins may be denying their own abilities, apathy, and over-dependence on men for their identity. Sins of this kind are not confined to women, of course. Harvey Cox suggests that 'man's' most serious sin 'is *not* his pride . . .it is his sloth, his unwillingness to be everything man was intended to be'. He continues, 'the traits of obedience, self-abnegation, docility, and forbearance can be expressions of sin.'[12]

But self-negation has been recognized by feminists as a key problem for women. The kind of caring work women perform often leaves them unable to consider their own needs. It is rewarding to do jobs which involve intensive care and service of others, but this can sap women's sense of individuality. Self-giving has to be balanced by personal flourishing, otherwise women end up giving themselves until nothing is left:

> Carers speak so often of 'being in second place', 'putting their own needs last' and so on, and it is easy to see that this self-denigration, loss of self-esteem and effacement is a concomitant of the caring role. If the carer has never had any attention paid to her needs and has had to carry on tending even when she herself is ill or would wish to be elsewhere, the end result is that she is a doormat, without ability to assert her own personality and make choices for herself. In the end, even the most normal of desires, for privacy, self-determination and respite, can seem to both dependant and carer as selfish and uncaring.[13]

Of course women can be selfish. But too often, they fail to value themselves or develop their capabilities fully, and are encouraged to believe that this self-denigration and self-sacrifice are virtuous. The ideals of the service ethic can lead them to feel that giving in the face of ingratitude, or devoting themselves to a small number of people, represents the height of virtue precisely because it is difficult to justify.

There is seldom proper analysis of the service women undertake, and serving others is regarded as virtuous whatever the conditions and motivation under which it is performed. Service-as-work is confused with service-as-love, and therefore takes on an emotional significance which makes it harder to do. Thus where serving the dinner on time is identified by King as an opportunity to lay down one's life for

Christ's sake, it ceases to be a routine task, but says 'I love God,' 'I love you,' 'I am a caring, self-denying and virtuous person.' The woman who fails to serve dinner on time has failed in all these other areas, and thus additional burdens are placed on her.

Although professional caring jobs incorporate a certain amount of detachment, where service-as-love is confused with service-as-work this is impossible. It becomes difficult to set limits and to stake out personal time when the person serving is unavailable. This is particularly true for women working in the home, but is also experienced by those in caring jobs which they do from a home base – clergy, or some doctors for example. When a request for help is refused, it is taken as a denial of love rather than recognized as legitimate limit-setting. Women's difficulties are made worse because they are emotionally involved with those for whom they care. Unlike clergy or doctors, women cannot shut the door after they have dealt with their 'clients'; when the door closes, their families are behind it with them.

A further difficulty is that Christian love is assumed not to require response or reward. Thus women's service work in the home is unpaid, and the service jobs in which women predominate are poorly paid. They may also be expected to serve without looking for any response from the one served, but this is unhelpful since to be the object of undiscriminating love is not an affirming experience, as I shall indicate. Moreover, if *all* that women do for others is viewed as service, offered because that is women's 'natural' role, they are robbed of the chance of freely offering service as love. When the service offered is expected or required, it cannot be identified with freely given love. Doing away with the expectation that a woman will iron her husband's shirts means she may, once in a while, be able to iron a shirt to show love. A similar dilemma is at the heart of some of the objections voiced by teachers. Whilst most are willing to do school work, attend meetings or be involved in out-of-school activities with pupils when it is their own choice, they feel aggrieved when these things are *required* of them as part of a job contract.

Anna Briggs has a useful discussion of these points for women: 'Though you can sometimes do something out of a sense of obligation,' she says, 'if an action is always carried out for this reason, or because of fear, eventually love goes out of it . . . the action becomes empty of meaning.' She continues: women 'learn that the creation and maintenance of love is our province and our duty. Our love is not to be given freely, but as part of the "contract" of a relationship.' But if love 'is natural for women it cannot be given freely; it is expected, only the absence of it will cause comment.' So women feel taken for granted, and this can turn to resentment:

> the givers often despise and resent the people whom they serve for not seeing the love behind the actions, for not reciprocating . . . Through a power structure and culture which sees women's selflessness as a natural characteristic, it is possible to avoid recognizing our actions as a conscious expression of love.[14]

The restrictions of the service ethic must be resisted because they frustrate that conscious expression of love, and prevent liberation, life and growth. That women are aware of the needs of others is no bad thing, but they need to know how to serve aright. It is when love and service and caring are identified with women's 'nature' that they become oppressive, as qualities shared by humankind they could be liberating. Women need 'to find new ways of co-operating with men in being *God's* servants on behalf of all humanity'. They need to be 'set free both to serve and to be served without loss of identity or fear of subordination'.[15] The next chapters begin to explore how this might happen.

· Chapter 8 ·

A love that makes others mature

Important note: if you live with a husband, be sure his conveniences are met first, that he has the largest closet, the most convenient space. All through the years this silently testifies that you care for him, that you're concerned about his needs first.[1]

To be loved and have literally nothing asked of one, and to be made to feel that there is no way in which one can ever give back anything of value, is to be made a pauper.[2]

The service ethic which underlies women's work is both destructive in its effects on women and on the people they serve, and prevents women from offering proper Christian service. We need to ask whether there is a more appropriate understanding of Christian love which can help women to serve God in their daily work.

A key feature of the love described in Chapter Three is that it does not look for reward or recognition. Clearly it would not be right to withhold love just because it is not appreciated properly, but true love *does* look for a response. This point is well made by Vanstone, who writes that 'love *needs*, though it does not *seek*, recognition: that it needs, for the completion of its work and for the good of the other, a recognition which it will by no means demand or compel'. When 'the other has grasped the meaning of its gifts and recognised them as symbols of love, then the work of love achieves its triumphant completion of self-giving'.[3] Love must be valued not according to how self-effacing it is, how little it asks for, but how demanding it is, how much response it expects.

Our love for others is modelled on God's love for us, and that *does* ask for a response. It is quite true that, as Christian tradition proclaims, God's love falls on everyone equally, and is undeserved. At particular stages in our lives we may welcome the knowledge that God loves us regardless of what we are like, that even the most miserable sinner is loved completely. Those who are conscious of great sinfulness are often helped by this emphasis. But it is not necessarily

69

appropriate for those who spend their lives looking after others and trying to serve God, yet feel worthless and have low self-esteem. The many women who fall into this category need to feel affirmed by God's love and stirred up to action, not told that it does not matter how worthless they are, because God loves them.

A wholly self-giving undemanding *agape* is unsatisfactory, for it calls for no response from us. This emphasis is in danger of being lost in Christian writings which stress that people's value is not dependent on what they do but on God's love. This is true as far as it goes, but it is not appropriate to make a complete separation between a person's worth and what they do. We are complex people, and want to feel that our whole selves are appreciated by those who love us. As Christians, we sometimes fall back on the idea that we should love others but are not called upon to like them. This may be a helpful way of encouraging us to show love to people who are thoroughly evil, but in general it is better that our loving should include liking. To be told 'I love you, but I do not like you' is deeply undermining; to know that someone likes, but does not love us, holds out hope that love might grow.

Insisting that true love should encompass liking is important, because it focuses attention on the individual who is to be loved. Love is not a 'thing' which is deposited on other people; it seeks to engage with what they are like, and get some response. Christian love values individuals by 'loving everyone in particular',[5] making each one feel valued and affirmed for themselves. Such affirmation is especially important for women, who frequently suffer from low self-esteem. While it may sound Christian to say 'I love you whatever you are like,' this may mean 'I do not really care what you are like.' Genuine love does care what the other is like, and will seek to change what is harmful or unlovable. God does not love us so that we can go on being worthless sinners, but in order that we might be changed. Whilst love is not conditional upon such changes, it must continue to look for a response.[4]

The fact that loving service is completed by receiving a response is important in the context of women's work. Many housewives complain that their families do not notice what they do, and they are frustrated by the lack of appreciation. This reaction can appear petty, but is in fact legitimate. Appreciation indicates that the meaning of the gift has been recognized. That is why the wives mentioned in Chapter One felt helped if their husbands voiced *awareness* of their problems or seemed willing to help, even if they did nothing. For they thereby appeared to recognize the unfair burden faced by their wives, and the women felt that their labours were appreciated. Where people serve for many years in a voluntary capacity in a church or other organization, they do not look for a reward. Yet public appreciation of what they have done may set the seal on their service.

The danger here is that people may feel that appreciating a service is a sufficient response. In some situations this may be the case, but it can mask injustice and hide the harsh character of the work being done. The idealization of mothers which takes place on Mother's Day illustrates this problem. It is as if telling mothers they are wonderful one day a year makes up for ignoring their hard work for the rest of the time. In the field of employment, women may be expected to serve more for the intrinsic rewards of the job itself than for the wages. Being thanked or idealized may take the place of a reasonable wage for the secretary or nurse, for example.

It might be that work which is done only for material benefit is inferior to work where there is a genuine wish to serve others. Some labour is alienated in the sense that workers have no opportunity to feel that they are contributing to the process, and theologians of work rightly urge that conditions should be changed in order to allow people to see their work as service. But this is quite different from suggesting that alienated labour can become joyous service simply because the worker does it for God.

It might be suggested that service must receive the *appropriate* recognition. In our society, value is generally expressed in financial terms. Being paid gives recognition to the value of the work done, and this is one reason why housewives feel devalued. Much is wrong with the present system, wage differentials are extreme and often bear little relation to the value of a piece of work to society as a whole. However, in principle it is reasonable to reward skills and to pay for services which are of value to society. It is not unchristian to receive a return for serving others. Reward for services may mean receiving a wage or can involve an exchange of labour such as might occur in a local community. People freely help one another when there are difficult circumstances, but in ordinary situations expect some reciprocation.

Many of the problems experienced by women in their service work arise because there is a mismatch between the response they expect or desire and what they actually receive. Women may perform a task with the intention of showing love, but find their service is taken for granted, and this leads to frustration. On the other hand, women may feel uneasy because they are idealized for performing tasks such as childcare, which they perceive as a duty.

Given the attitudes towards women in our society, it is difficult to alleviate this problem. Women have to be seen not as saints but as human beings, with all the virtues and vices humanity shares. One way of enabling this to happen is for women to learn to articulate their needs and motivations. If a loving act only receives its full meaning when it is recognized, it may be necessary to draw attention to what has been done and why. Christians may instinctively feel that this is contrary to the gospel, believing that to draw attention to a good work is to devalue it. In some situations it may be appropriate for good works to be performed anonymously; but in the context of a relationship love needs to declare itself. For example, children who learn many years later that their mother sacrificed her health in order to look after all their needs are likely to respond: 'Why did we not know?' Oppenheimer's point is relevant here: that to be unable to respond or give anything in return for loving service is to be made a pauper.

Clearly, to have a response *demanded* of one may be damaging. Where service is undertaken only in order to gain love or gratitude it can lead to emotional blackmail, and this is the basis of the stereotype of the possessive mother. It is actually a form of domination, not service, and is very destructive: 'Not even Jesus came to fetter human beings to himself by his ministry, to make himself indispensable for them.'[6] Service and sacrifice need to be made visible in a way which leaves others free to respond or to reject. This is the model offered us by Christ, who does not compel recognition of his sacrifice, yet whose work would be meaningless if people were unable to understand and respond to his life, death and resurrection. The service offered by Christ did not make him subordinate to other people, but was a free offering of himself, with an acceptance of service and love in return.

Just as service does not have to forgo a return in order to be Christian, so it does not have to be unlimited. Many problems arise when people are not able to have time off, or have to work in poor conditions. It is particularly difficult for women working at home to set limits around what they do, but it is not unchristian for them to do so. Indeed, without proper limits both their own health and the efficiency of the task being done would suffer. If housework and childcare are important, though unpaid jobs, they need to be done under fair conditions. Some Christian writers do recognize this, and suggest that women should take time off. In paid work, insisting on reasonable wages and fair conditions is a matter of justice. Because women's jobs often involve personal service of others, it can be as difficult for them to set limits in their employment as it is in the home. Thus secretaries often find that people do not treat their work seriously, interrupting breaks or getting papers to them late. They are expected to perform tasks which are not strictly part of their jobs, yet if they refuse, they appear obstinate and unpleasant.

A love which recognizes others as individuals may be more difficult to practise than the spontaneous, uncalculating , unconditional love of which Nygren speaks, for it must exercise discernment over how love is shown. Thus Ferré writes:

> The nature of love is to bestow freedom on the other while still having complete concern for him *(sic)*. Merely to let live is not love. Always to do for the other . . . is not love. Agape is complete concern for the other while allowing him to be genuinely free. Therefore agape acts or refrains from acting according to the need of the other.[7]

Christian service, then, may mean refusing to meet a particular need, for the sake of others. But the motive for withholding service is love, a concern for the flourishing of all those involved. We need to learn, in Moltmann-Wendel's terms, 'a love that makes others mature.'[8]

If service is important, it must be a capability taught to both sexes and all ages. This may mean not doing things for other people, to enable them to develop a sense of responsibility for themselves. In families, every member has an equal responsibility to consider the needs of others. If it is always left to one person, usually the woman, to be sensitive to what is needed, no one else learns that skill. One of the greatest services women might perform for sons or husbands in particular is *not* to do everything for them.

Women may find it difficult to state their own needs and give others the chance to serve and minister to them. One woman cared for a succession of needy people in her home. But when she herself grew old and in need of care, she repeatedly said: 'I don't want to be a bother to people.' This feeling may be because women put too low a value on themselves, and this point is discussed below. But it is also important to make others aware of one's own needs as part of the lesson of mutual responsibility.

This insight is illustrated by 'Val', in her caring for her elderly disabled mother. At first she saw herself 'as a cross between Florence Nightingale and an early Christian martyr – nursing and caring for my mother, keeping the home spotless, washing, ironing, cooking, shopping, gardening, yet always available with a sympathetic ear and practical help for my husband and sons . . . and of course, always smiling bravely!' Accepting that this was not realistic, and that her own needs were important, was a stepping-stone for growth. The elderly should not be shielded from the reality of the tiredness and unrealistic demands they make, any more than should children, she writes. As she and her mother worked on enabling the mother to do more for herself, the situation was greatly improved.[9]

Many women find it extremely difficult to receive service from others, and are reluctant to ask for help. This relates partly to the ideology of coping, for women feel they ought to manage on their own. When 'Granny' in Posy Simmonds' cartoon comes in and does a lot of extra housework, it may seem to imply that she is criticizing the current state of the house. It is also difficult to accept, because it puts the recipients under an obligation not of their choosing. Posy Simmonds captures Wendy Weber's ambivalent feelings of guilt, gratitude and annoyance in this situation.

Reluctance to accept service can also be connected with low self-esteem, and a feeling that we do not deserve to be helped. Yet a relaxed acceptance that others wish to serve us can be liberating for those who are usually givers. Genuine thankfulness to others not only enriches our own lives through their gift, but gives them the pleasure of giving freely. It is a false humility which is always saying 'You shouldn't have bothered,' or 'I'm sorry to inconvenience you,' not only in our relationship with other people but also with God. If we continually tell God how worthless we are and how little we merit salvation, we are unlikely to grow in our Christian lives. It is as if we are stuck at the first stage of becoming a Christian. Instead, we need to accept God's gift of love and let it enrich our lives as we move forward to spiritual maturity.

It may seem that where another person is in need, the Christian is under an obligation to meet that need. But not all needs have the same priority, and the nature of the need must be evaluated alongside consideration of the appropriate response to it. It makes sense for women to ask what is the purpose of the particular sacrifices they are making. Since no individual can meet all the needs with which they

are confronted, it is necessary to establish priorities. Women have assumed that serving children and husband is their most important task, and they are encouraged in this belief by some Christian writers. Thus King says that women who are mothers should concentrate on this, since 'taking care of our children is the Lord's work . . . the day-by-day constant caring for . . . children (is) . . . accomplishing something great in the kingdom of God'. She adds: 'We are adding a greater burden to society than we could ever compensate for with all our good deeds if we don't spend time training our children or if we don't spend time helping them to be secure as people.'[10]

It is questionable whether this is literally true, but even if it were, it would apply equally to fathers. Most people have obligations towards their families which they must fulfil, both to provide physical care and emotional nurturing. Society rightly puts pressure on people to fulfil their responsibilities, since children or disabled relatives must not be neglected. But this does not mean that such care must be the sole province of women. Responsibilities can be discharged in a variety of ways. Women need to evaluate their caring work critically, rather than assuming any sacrificial service is worthwhile.

Janet Radcliffe Richards discusses this point in depth. She notes that whilst the work of a housewife may use some of her particular gifts, 'domestic work cannot make the best use of the abilities of any highly able woman, and few achievements of any housewife are comparable with what a gifted woman could achieve outside'. She takes issue with the suggestion that looking after children is the most worthwhile work anyone can do. For, she says, if it is valuable to bring up your own children properly, it is even more valuable to make sure all children are brought up properly: 'if it is important to see that your children get a good education, it is even better to make sure that the whole school system works well'.[11]

Women, she says, must consider how their energies might best be used , for 'a decision to devote oneself to the service of someone else, with no consideration of whether he is worth serving or whether something else is more worth doing, is not the highest goodness but a total abnegation of morality'. Of course women should be willing to make sacrifices when this *is* the best thing to do. Women may reasonably be suspicious when their sacrifices seem only to foster the comfort and status of men.[12]

The difficulty in our present situation is that so many women are forced to choose between caring properly for their own children and using their abilities fully in the wider sphere. It is important, however, for women to consider what they should be doing, and not take refuge in the idea that all women belong in the domestic sphere, regardless of their personality and attributes. Despite the importance of family responsibilities, in the end these are superseded by the claims of the gospel.

A willingness to make sacrifices is important, but we must be wary lest this condones injustice. True goodness cannot tolerate tyranny, and Christians need to confront suffering rather than accept it passively. The Christian has a duty to fight against injustice for the sake of those who are oppressed by it. However, it is not always possible for the oppressed to take this stand. Women are frequently oppressed by their labour, exploited and unable to break free because of their powerlessness. In this context the assertion that Christians must fight such oppression has little relevance, for to resist can mean losing one's livelihood or causing others to suffer. Nevertheless, it is important for Christians to say that such a situation is wrong, even if it has to be accepted temporarily because there is no way out. Accepting injustice as a personal share in the sufferings of Christ ignores the responsibility each Christian has to the rest of humankind. We do others a disservice when we allow them to carry on with oppression without challenging what they are doing.

One of our models of Christ is the Suffering Servant, the Lamb who is dumb before its shearers. Yet Christ himself gets angry and enters into conflict. In the New Testament, the Lamb is also wrathful. We need to accept that anger can be constructive, and can help us to break free from what oppresses us, as Campbell points out. It is important to 'name the enemy', so that people can move from a diffuse sense of anger and helplessness to a 'direct and unashamed expression of what they want from others, especially from those closest to them'.[13] This is especially difficult for women, given the mechanisms which prevent them expressing their anger. Assertiveness training for women is one response to this need. It is designed to help them to express their feelings and desires in a reasonable and non-aggressive fashion. It is essential to be clear about needs if change is to take place.

Christianity has traditionally approved of those who renounce their rights, their privileges and their family relationships for the sake of the gospel. There is a place for personal sacrifice of this kind, although it must take account of the effect this can have upon others. In the context of work, workers might take a wage cut in order to help a company in financial difficulties, or mothers might accept having no time to themselves whilst their children are small babies. The point here, however, is that there is an element of choice. It is recognized that under normal conditions workers have a right to a fair wage, or mothers to time off.

There is thus a distinction to be made between what is done freely and what is done under obligation. It is inappropriate to equate forced sacrifice with a genuine act of service. According to the service ethic, the Christian worker ceases to see the obligatory character of work, so that what was formerly done 'as sheer necessity, or . . . out of a sense of duty . . . is now done "unto the Lord", and becomes joyous and free service'.[14] Women may say that their housework ceases to be a chore when they become Christians, because it is now done for Christ. Yet the fact remains that most work *is* obligatory, and remains so whatever the spirit in which it is done. Christian service does not mean pretending that work about which we have no choice is really 'joyous and free service'. Work is 'good work' because it contributes to the flourishing of God's creation, not because it is done 'for the Lord', or done by Christians. George Herbert is mistaken to assert that 'Who sweeps a room as for thy laws/Makes that and the action fine', unless sweeping the room is a worthwhile action in the context. If a job involves drudgery and alienation, and is dehumanizing, then Christians must struggle to change conditions.

Christians have sometimes talked as if true love and service can only be offered by Christians. A doctor in *Just the Job* reports a concern amongst some Christian doctors as to 'how to shine when our non-Christian colleagues are clever, hard-working and compassionate', perhaps even more so than the Christians.[15] Clearly the ability to serve others aright is not confined to Christians. Many women sacrifice themselves for others without seeking any reward, and many of them are not Christians. Neither can we suggest that the love shown by Christians has a special quality, for again, equal or even greater love for others can be found amongst non-Christians. There is a human desire to relate in love to one another which reflects the God in whose image we are made. It might be that Christians are more likely to show that love, but what is essentially different is the context in which we set our service. For Christians, it will be a means of maturing a relationship with God, and a means of fulfilment and flourishing.

As Christians, we are called to serve by our faith, and Christ urges his followers to go beyond what is normally expected. But this kind of love cannot be engineered; it is a response which springs, for Christians, out of our relationship with Christ. Christianity requires that we love even our enemies with a genuine and all-encompassing love. But it also allows us to recognize that such love can never be perfectly achieved. Though made in the image of God, we can only imperfectly mirror God's love. Our relationships with one another are distorted, and it is difficult for care and affection to be properly reciprocal. This particularly seems to be the case with the relationships between the sexes.

Acknowledging the imperfections of human love is important, for it introduces a necessary note of realism into the debate. Women have suffered through being idealized, as if mothers or wives were able to satisfy all the needs, both material and emotional, of their husbands or children. Inevitably they fail, but if we can recognize that no human being can provide perfect care for another, we can free women to be appreciated for doing the best they can. In the end it is God alone who is the source of perfect love: 'There is a mother who lives up to our hopes, though we are not she.'[16]

The realization that sin distorts service should lead us to be careful how we speak of it. There is ambivalence in service. Genuine attempts to show love through service can easily lead to the problems of the service ethic. Actions which do spring from love may be misunderstood, and this is particularly likely to happen where women withhold their service. Yet loving in a way that makes others mature will always be risky. It involves interacting with others, looking for a response which may not come. It requires that we consider what our service is doing to others, both individually and in society. Serving God and others aright is a demanding and challenging road to follow.

· *Chapter 9* ·

Living first for God's sake

> Because she is the glory of man and marks the completion of his creation, it is not problematical but self-evident for her to be ordained for man and to be for man in her whole existence . . . She would not be woman if she had even a single possibility apart from being man's helpmeet.[1]

> I wish woman to live *first* for God's sake. Then she will not make an imperfect man her god, and thus sink to idolatry. Then she will not take what is not fit for her from a sense of weakness and poverty. Then if she finds what she needs in Man embodied, she will know how to live and be worthy of being loved.[2]

Self-fulfilment has been highly valued in Western society in recent years. An emphasis on self-help and overcoming misfortune has a positive side, but it can deny the importance of caring for others. Self-fulfilment as a goal can only work in a harmonious world where people's ideals do not conflict. This is where theology has a contribution to make, because it takes disharmony and sin very seriously. It also reminds us that some people are fulfilled through evil actions, and so must not be allowed to do as they wish.

Nevertheless, given the low expectations many women have of themselves, encouragement to fulfil and advance themselves can have a positive effect. There is an emphasis on fulfilment in many recent books for Christian women. Women are said to be privileged to have a unique and glorious role in the world, the home and the Church, and are to use their talents. For Mitson, women are essentially creative. She observes truly that women are too 'absorbed in giving themselves in service to others, to have time to use their creative gifts in the way that they would like to'.[3] But their creative gifts are to be extended only in the domestic and personal spheres: 'We are all creative beings, and we have been created in God's image . . . We create either a good impression or a bad impression . . . a warm welcoming environment or a cold unfriendly one'.[4] Women are told to honour God by 'looking good'. Brawn writes: 'Of course God judges us by what happens in

80

our hearts, but . . . he wants to redeem every area of our lives, including the way we dress'.[5]

Similarly, where women are urged to develop themselves, it is likely to be for the benefit of other people. Reeves says that

> A woman owes it to her husband to be an attractive, interesting and informed companion as well as a homemaker and spiritual partner, and she certainly owes it to herself not to let her personality be submerged by the demands of bringing up a family. One day she may find herself living alone.[6]

Whilst women are in relationships, their energy should be used for the benefit of others; it is only when women are single that they can concentrate on themselves.

A considerable amount of material for Christian women gives practical advice on their looks and on ways of running a home. In many respects this parallels the advice given in popular women's magazines, except that Christian women look good for God. Some of the suggestions are potentially useful. For example, King and Ortlund recommend principles of time management and organization which can indeed aid women in their daily lives. But for all the glorification of woman's role, the fact remains that it is a limited one. Despite acknowledgement that some women do have useful careers, their prime work is in the home and in supporting male leadership. A sharp distinction is made between women's calling to mundane activity and men's calling to creative mastery of the world; what Comer describes as 'making men climb mountains and women climb stairs and making grown men put away childish things and women put away children's things'.[7]

Discussions of creativity for men are more likely to stress their responsibilities over the earth. Brett describes the importance of creativity:

> The growth of science and technology, affording man ever-increasing control of the universe, are the proper outworking of this creative urge . . . Man can even be seen to be bringing about the redemption of the world through his work in it, humanising it as he masters it and brings it into subjection to himself.'[8]

Theoretically and theologically, 'man' here includes 'woman'. But this is not the language usually used when specifically speaking about women. Indeed, to speak of woman controlling the universe through

81

science and technology, bringing it into subjection to herself, is to make a challenging statement about women's role in the world.

Despite the fact that it is both sexes together who are commanded to have dominion over the world,[9] it is common for different roles to be assigned. Oldham, for example, asks whether 'work conceived as the technical mastery of the external world is not specifically a male interest and whether the activities characteristic of woman's essential nature do not lie in a different field'.[10] Brand, considering the command to have dominion, says: 'Where men are to rule the direction of life, women are to rule its quality. Whereas men provide leadership, women provide atmosphere. Whereas men control the choices, women control the environment.'[11] This once again reflects the idea that women are bearers of goodness who influence men's actions by their spiritual, sensitive 'nature'.

It is of course problematic to speak of women's 'essential nature', and in any case, women might be commanded to expand their horizons from what comes 'naturally' to them. Women's creativity takes many different forms, as does men's, and they need to be given the opportunity to use it for their own fulfilment and for the good of society. Women whose gifts lie outside the traditional confines often meet with disapproval. Whilst there is lip-service paid in the Church to the idea that some women have a vocation to the single life, single women often feel excluded. Christians emphasize 'The Family', and woman's role within it, so that women who do not marry or have children present the Church with a problem.

The stereotypes of single men and women portray happy, carefree bachelors and frustrated spinsters. Yet in reality, marriage suits men better than women. Jessie Bernard wrote in 1973 that 'there are few findings more consistent, less equivocal, more convincing, than the sometimes spectacular and always impressive superiority on almost every index . . . of married over never married men'.[12] Men can find no better guarantor of long life, happiness and health than finding a wife to look after them, whilst women are more likely to find these things if they remain unmarried, she writes.

These findings would need to be examined again for the 1980s, but it is likely that the trend would be the same. Marriage for women brings with it a role which restricts their opportunities. Simply being a wife probably has less effect today, since chores are more likely to be shared between wife and husband. But once children arrive, women usually find much heavier responsibilities in the home, and an expectation that being a wife and mother is henceforward their main role. Many women welcome this, despite finding particular aspects of it oppressive. But the key point is whether they have any choice over what they do. Some degree of self-fulfilment is necessary for both sexes if they are to grow as human beings. Having some control over one's own life, and some measure of independence, is good for people's mental health. That is why the most stressful jobs are those which give great responsibilities with little control over working conditions.

Clearly, most people have only a limited number of options from which to choose, and seldom feel completely in control of their own destinies. Individual choice needs to be balanced against the needs of society, and the most desirable jobs or roles will always have limited availability. But choice can still be exercised within these limitations. Women generally are restricted in the choices available to them. For many women across the world, the question of choice is irrelevant. Simply enabling their families to survive takes all their energy. Women in industrialized societies have many privileges, yet even here their opportunities for self-development are more limited than men's. The range of jobs women do is narrower than men's, and the emphasis on self-denying service of others, whilst sometimes fulfilling, also gives rise to the problems of the service ethic. As Sharpe points out: 'Almost all the careers for women that involve intensive care and service of others contain the implicit contradiction that the very aspect of the job that makes it worthwhile can also wear away or suffocate women's sense of individuality.'[13]

The fact that self-sacrifice is understood as a normal component of women's role means that they have little choice about it. Too often, where women do have a choice the alternatives are unrealistic and unsatisfactory. For example, as we saw in Chapter Four, women (but not men) are told that if they wish to have children they should stay at home to look after them full time; either a career or children, but not both. Indeed, women's desire for small changes in their lives tends to be exaggerated into impossible choices which bear little relation to the original request. Thus the suggestion that women do not need to be treated with deference – having doors held open for them, or given seats on buses – results in no consideration being shown at all. The choice is either to admit male superiority and be treated with kindness, or affirm the equality of the sexes and be left to struggle alone when in difficulties.

These are not the choices that women would choose to give themselves, and being offered them presents women with new difficulties. Those who describe the tensions generated by departure from traditional roles, have a point. It is easier when fixed roles are followed, as Dally shows:

> In our present world of choice the majority of women are not educated to make choices, do not wish to choose, and frown on their sisters who do. The fact that there is so much choice either frightens them consciously or drives them to hide from it and try to find a way of life that ignores choice.

It is, she adds, 'difficult to feel a sense of achievement in coping with difficulties and miseries if others think you brought them on yourself or could choose to step out of them altogether'. Thus many women 'felt more secure in being certain that they were the weaker sex than in being aware that they are not'.[14]

Yet growth involves having some choice in and control over one's own life. As Christians we may then choose to serve Christ, and give control of our lives to God. But this is a proper response to God's gift of freedom, *choosing* whom we will serve, not being forced to do the will of others: 'Liberation does not mean that we can all do only what we please all the time. It means that our choices are made in the light of our responsibility to God's Kingdom, not in response to social pressures and stereotypes.'[15] The essence of moral decision is choice, and accepting responsibility for that choice. If women feel they have no choice, they may also excuse themselves from responsibility. If a characteristic sin of women is to avoid their responsibility for independent action in the world, then they need to be encouraged to make independent choices.

This is recognized in general by many Christian writers, but rarely applied to both sexes. It is also more common to find men being urged to fulfil their potential than women. Catherwood writes that 'it is the duty of the Christian to use his abilities to the limit of his physical and mental capacity . . . He has a duty to train himself and develop his abilities . . . to the limit that his other responsibilities allow.'[16] For the theologian Karl Barth, Woman is not to find herself through choice but 'chooses herself by refraining from choice; by finding herself surrounded and sustained by the joyful choice of the man, as his elect'. Barth does not believe this involves 'anything strange, or humiliating, or detrimental, or restrictive of the true humanity of woman',[17] but this is simply not true. To be denied any opportunity to choose for oneself is destructive whichever sex is involved.

Scanzoni and Hardesty comment that:

> Self-actualization for women is discouraged in much Christian writing. Somehow women are supposed to be different from men, being able to live through someone else (husband, children) and to find their fulfilment through self-effacement and vicarious experiences rather than through direct participation in the world. When women complain about this and ask to be able to achieve as men do, they're called 'selfish' and are told they are rebelling against God.[18]

Women are half the human race, and like men are made in God's image with many and varied God-given talents. The gospel calls both women and men to follow Christ, use their talents, and to act responsibly and creatively in the world. However important it is for women to take their responsibilities as wives and mothers seriously, all Christians are called to serve the Body of Christ with whatever gifts they have. Both sexes will be judged if they have wasted their talents: 'Regardless of the structures of society or the church which stand in our way, our calling in Christ is to use the gifts God has given us as co-partners in Christ's work, so that God's will is done on earth as it is in heaven.'[19]

What Christian women need is, in Scanzoni and Hardesty's words, to be

> free to give the world all that our individual talents, minds, and personalities have to offer. . . We ask for the right to make our own choices, to define our own lives, not out of selfish motivations but because God calls us and commands us to develop the gifts he has given us.[20]

Although these gifts may be used in marriage and the raising of a family, such relationships cannot be an end in themselves. Christ himself came not to bring peace but a sword, to set sons against fathers, daughters against mothers. Whoever loves father, mother or children more than Christ is not fit to be his disciple.[21]

Throughout Christian history there have been women who have chosen another path than marriage and family life, in order that they might follow their Christian calling. Women are supported in this by the model of sainthood in the Catholic tradition. This has its problems, but does at least contradict the message that women's Christian vocation demands a total sacrifice of their lives for husband and children. Individual women have left husband or children 'for the sake of the gospel', but this is not easy for Christians to accept. There is an expectation that men's relationships will take second place to their vocations – many clergy wives suffer from this. Thus it would be difficult to take C.S. Lewis's words seriously for women:

> In the last resort, we must turn down or disqualify our nearest and dearest when they come between us and our obedience to God. Heaven knows, it will seem to them sufficiently like hatred. We must not act on the pity we feel; we must be blind to tears and deaf to pleadings.[22]

The parallel between Lewis's words and those of Adrienne Rich in Chapter Seven is striking, and not coincidental. For whilst a common Christian criticism of feminism is that it encourages women to reject their family relationships, the gospel, too, has this implication. For women to stop being completely available to service men's needs, and to cease treating them as children, is a response to God's calling to both sexes to grow into mature adulthood.

Nonetheless, although the Christian's priority is to serve God rather than family or friends, in most cases the two should not conflict. For we serve God in partnership, and through meeting our responsibilities to one another. In the present climate, where sacrificial service is deemed to be women's priority, it is right to stress the need for fulfilment. But in fact good relationships are vital if women are to grow, just as they must have a secure sense of self if they are to love others aright. The fact that women are sensitive to the needs of others is good. It is only problematic because women's own needs are not recognized, and they may find it difficult to receive care from another even where it is offered.

Dependency is a basic human need, since people have to be confident that they can depend on others if they are to be independent. As Posy Simmonds shows, even the worriers need someone to worry about them. Eichenbaum and Orbach point out that women are stereotyped as dependent, and learn to *behave* dependently. Yet women are also 'raised to be depended *upon* for emotional support and nurturance.'[23] Men have their emotional dependency needs catered for more consistently than do women, first by their mothers then by wives or other women. Because of this, men

may not appreciate that they have such needs, and that it is this which enables them to be more independent. Girls learn early on that there is no one to take care of them emotionally. Their dependency needs are not sufficiently tended to, and so they look for this in their relationships. If women look to their children for emotional nurturance, it can be crippling for the child. What women need is to have good adult relationships, since 'it is only through satisfaction of our dependency needs and the security of loving and nurturing relationships which provide us with an emotional anchor that we can truly feel autonomous'.[24]

It is of profound theological importance that we recognize the connections between independence and relationship. The model for this may be found in parental love, which at its best fulfils the emotional dependency needs of children, but strives to achieve their independence. It has expectations of children and looks for reciprocation. God's love for us is like this, and the picture of God who loves us as a parent is found throughout Scripture. We are cared for tenderly, judged when we do wrong, forgiven, urged to grow up, and to love in return.

Our human relationships will be strongest where they follow this pattern. We must resist the idea that the normal expressions of family relationships need to be replaced by self-sacrificial *agape* which looks for no return. Our adult relationships ideally involve interdependence and reciprocation, and a concern to make the other mature. At times this will include gentle nurturing, but this will not be in one direction only, nor will it be the pattern for the entire relationship.

Creativity and using talents to the full are important areas to stress for women. The objection that these are selfish and unchristian ideals arises from the misconception that self-fulfilment and service are always opposed to one another. An emphasis on mutual love helps to avoid this polarization, and this is the theme of the final chapter.

· Chapter 10 ·

Not nervous of being made happy

Servitude . . . of this sort is a gift of God. Wherefore compliance with this servitude is to be reckoned among blessings.[1]

(Women) have made too many of the wrong sacrifices; they have been guilty of a suicide of personality. For too long Christians and Christian women have confused free sacrifice, service, and obedience with passivity, servility, and self-destructive acquiescence.[2]

One of the key questions posed for Christians is whether they will follow their own inclinations or submit to Christ. The 'natural' self is portrayed as strong and selfish, needing to be denied in order to allow Christ-like qualities to grow. But whilst this is one way of seeing our Christian lives, it is not always the most appropriate emphasis for women. It offers them the unhelpful choice between attention to their own needs *or* service of others. In Christian literature for women, the choice is between being hard, selfish and unfeminine, or soft, responsive and a beautiful woman. If 'the characteristic tendency of woman as a sinner is to be self-willed',[3] as Marshall suggests, it would be right to direct them away from their own desires. But since women's sin is more likely to be self-negation, condemning their impulses to self-fulfilment only compounds their problems.

For many Christians, seeking self-fulfilment and making demands on others are products of a sinful self-love. Nygren writes that 'Christianity does not recognize self-love as Christian', for it 'blocks the channels of self-spending and self-offering, both towards God and towards man'.[4] But other theologians suggest that there is a right self-love, and Oppenheimer is particularly helpful here. She explains that to learn to put God first, others second, and self last 'is so far from being the answer to our problems that it is itself our problem'. If we knew how to put God first, we would be 'home already', and 'for most of us, the conscious attempt to put self last could make us at best difficult to live with and at worst eaten up with spiritual pride'.[5]

89

In any case, she says, self-denial can never be an end in itself, since if 'any creatures are to be loved and cherished, then sooner or later we ourselves are likewise to be loved and cherished'. If we love other people as ourselves, we must cope with the fact that they will be likely to love us as themselves. Our fulfilment and theirs need not and should not be separated. It is, says Oppenheimer, an insult to God and our fellows to treat *ourselves* negatively; we cannot opt out of being lovable. If we ourselves are to be loved and cherished, then self-fulfilment must be important. Talking about self-giving as something entirely separate from fulfilment does not do justice either to God's love or human love. What we need is 'a love that is not nervous of being made happy'.[6]

This is an important point, since for women in particular, self-giving has been set against self-fulfilment. As we saw earlier, this is the case for 'working mothers', whose desire for employment is seen as contradicting the needs of their children, although little attention is paid to their actual situation. This conflict between self and others is a central problem for women. In many circumstances there seems to be no way of resolving the tension without either totally sacrificing themselves or appearing unpleasantly self-centred. Acting independently and caring for others are not mutually exclusive, however, for neither is possible without the other. One cannot give from emptiness, and neither selfish fulfilment nor self-negation are satisfying.

The key, to use Oppenheimer's terms once again, is 'flourishing'.[7] This is an important concept, for it reflects how we think about God. Rather than seeing God in purely negative terms, as the one who judges and punishes our sins, the goal of human flourishing encourages us to remember that creativity, joy and an affirming love are fundamental to God's character. An emphasis on self-denial may lead Christians to feel that if they enjoy anything it must be wrong. But if we are created to grow and flourish, delight must have a place in our lives. Women have often been unwilling to foster this in themselves, and the circumstances of their lives may make it difficult for them to do so. But even within these constraints, women can start by owning what gives them pleasure. It causes difficulties when women feel they must recast their 'selfish' motives as altruistic. Thus a woman may cook an elaborate meal because she enjoys cooking, but present it to her family as if they required such a high standard. If her family did not want that meal, they will be unappreciative and resent her for making them feel guilty. If the woman can admit that she performed the task for her own pleasure, she will not require any other return, although she will be glad if her family share her pleasure.

This emphasis on the self may seem unchristian, for Christianity teaches that fulfilment comes *through* service – of Christ and others – and that it is those who lose their lives who find them. But for this to happen, people need to have a self to lose, a personality to give to others. Too often women have put aside their personal development as they have concentrated on serving others. Many claim that they are fulfilled. Those who accept the model of true Christian womanhood described in earlier chapters may find great satisfaction in submitting to male authority and trying to create a positive environment. Life may indeed seem peaceful and fulfilling, although for every woman whose Christian success story is upheld, there are others who feel guilty, frustrated, worthless and unspiritual.

Those who advocate this way of life accept that it does not always work out in practice, but insist that it is God's plan. Brand says:

> God is the originator of this mystery of submission and authority, and he is well able to bring about his will in our lives no matter who else appears to be making a mess of things. As far as I am concerned, the deep peace of doing it his way outweighs all the petty disturbances of human errors of judgement.[8]

It is quite true that God's way appears to be foolish at times, and is not easy to follow. But we cannot assume that every option which appears foolish is therefore God's will. Generally speaking, God's will for our lives is firmly based on what is functional for us as individuals and for human society as a whole. If strict role differentiation or female subordination cause frustration and unhappiness, and prevent people from offering God and the world all that they are and can do, then it is difficult to see how they can be part of the Kingdom of God.

Instead of taking the submissive woman as God's model disciple, we might do well to heed Russell's warning that submission 'is in fact an element of sinfulness in which women refuse to accept their full created status as partners with men in the work of God's mission in the world'.[9] God's love liberates both women and men for flourishing and creative service. We are to use every talent we are given freely, not hold back because our gifts do not fit stereotyped notions of masculinity or femininity, or because we think God has prescribed fixed roles for the sexes.

It is crucial for women's calling as disciples that they reject the idea that service of others and self-fulfilment must always be opposed to each other, for God's love encompasses both. Instead we must challenge the social attitudes and organization which force women to choose between their own well-being and their responsibilities to others. If women are to love and serve others, then they too must be loved and served. Self-fulfilment and self-giving are closely related. We are able to serve others without being subservient because our own interests and those of others are inextricably bound together. All of us are to partake of the flourishing which is the hallmark of God's Kingdom.

This assertion may sound idealistic, since in a fallen world interests inevitably conflict. However, it is important to make a common flourishing our goal, rather than calling Christian a solution which favours the interests of one side and takes no account of the cost to the other. Men have not experienced a conflict between self and others in quite the same way as women, yet it is important for them, too, to be able to harmonize service and self-affirmation. Both sexes need to find ways of being whole people, discovering how to be both creative and loving in work and relationships.

When women do not feel they have to oppose self-giving and self-fulfilment, they are more easily able to state their own needs. Women have traditionally valued personal relationships, although this has sometimes been regarded as a weakness. But only if women's emotional needs are properly met will they be able to play their full part in the world. It can be argued that self-fulfilment is not possible without the mutual support of others. Women who are isolated, whether in traditionally male jobs or within the home, need bonds with other women. As they discover a common perception of oppression, women are enabled to tackle sexism effectively; and feminism makes a powerful contribution here.

But equally, women need their bonds with men to be transformed. Liberation will not be complete unless women are able to serve men, as well as receive service in return. Men and women need to acknowledge their dependency needs, and discover how these can best be met without one partner exploiting or manipulating the other. Both sexes need to recognize the humanity which they share, rather than projecting on to the other undesirable or idealized qualities. Once again, it is this emphasis on our common humanity which points the way forward:

92

when women do not need to live through their husband and children, men will not fear the love and strength of women, nor need another's weakness to prove their own masculinity. They can finally see each other as they are . . . Who knows of the possibilities of love when men and women share not only children, home, and garden, not only the fulfilment of their biological roles, but the responsibilities and passions of the work that creates the human future?[10]

The central contention of this book is that women's lives are constricted by the application of a service ethic, which demands that they serve others sacrificially, without complaint and without reward. Whilst women do wish to contribute to society, a different emphasis is required for them. It is not enough to stress the importance of service without exploring the content of the word. It must include a discussion of what service means in different circumstances, and relate this to the political and social dimensions which have been obscured in the past by its confusion with sacrificial love.

This does not mean that women should completely cease from sacrificing themselves in the service of others. But it needs to be a considered service, not something which is slipped into because that is the feminine role. Some service is demanded of us by family relationships, or in our jobs; but if we have *chosen* that caring job, or *chosen* to play a caring role in our families, our service can be genuine and free. Women who find they are expected to serve others simply because they are women, wives or mothers, and regardless of their own situation, may feel frustrated. Given the choice, many women would probably wish to spend their lives caring for others. But they need to do this on very different terms from the present conditions.

Firstly, women's caring needs to be complemented by men's caring, not to exclude it. As a society we need men to develop their nurturing qualities for use not just within their own families but in the wider world. Secondly, taking on caring responsibilities, whether at home or in employment, should not be seen as taking on board the service ethic. The choice to care for a disabled relative, or to be at home with small children, should not be met with the argument: 'You chose to do this yourself; you should suffer the consequences.' Rather, we should be asking: 'What support do you need to enable you to carry on with the service you have undertaken?' Even with support, some sacrifices will have to be made, but most women will not mind this. What matters 'is not that there should be no sacrifices, but that they should be fairly distributed, honestly recognized and not allowed to become outrageous'.[11]

Freely making sacrifices for others is part of the way in which we find fulfilment, and this is something Christians must continue to stress. Roger Clarke does not sufficiently take into account the problems of service, particularly for women, but once we have established what service should mean, his 'Contribution Ethic' is useful:

> a belief that our humanity does find fulfilment in doing things for others. That God is glorified through our being of service to our fellows whether that be through employee/customer relationships in the paid economy or whether that service, that giving of ourselves, is manifested . . . quite outwith the paid economy.[12]

If we can define work in general as 'doing things for others', we can see that women's service does not have a special character. It is work like any other. We have to resist attributing special value to the tasks women perform, just as we must resist labelling the feminine as virtuous. Women's work, like men's work, is good where it builds up relationships, whether the task is undertaken in the community, the factory or the home. Christians have often seen jobs which directly serve others as more Christian than, for example, work in industry. Yet both are necessary for the building up of human society:

> Our calling is to obediently serve in the healing, renewing, and unfolding of God's good creation; to love God, to live before his face in praying, raising children, doing justice, making chairs, building, playing, eating, sleeping; to do all things to his honour and glory.[13]

For women to share fully in this vocation, they need to be freed from being prescribed only a narrow range of roles, and need to be encouraged to develop their capabilities in the context which is most appropriate for them. All Christians are to develop their full potential and take responsibility over creation, and this issues a challenge to women who have previously seen their role as essentially supportive and 'expressive'. When women take these responsibilities seriously, they bring to them a concern for human relations which has often been missing in the masculine world-view. Women might wish to emphasize human relationships as another means by which humankind shares in the creativity of God. This is not to argue that women 'by nature' are caring, whilst men are not. We have already seen that such statements are problematic. But women have learnt the value of nurturance and the importance of human relationships with each other and with creation, and need to share this with men.

A statement that women must take responsibility over creation does not imply that every individual woman must do work which has an impact on the wider world. It is possible to fulfil one's potential within the family or a local community, although there are points where responsibility to society at large will be exercised. Individual women may be quite right to work full time in the home if they so choose. What must be objected to is the idea that this is the proper role for all women, and the one through which they contribute the greatest good to society.

If people require elements of choice in, and control over, their lives in order to grow, prescribed roles and strict role differentiation are counter-productive. If our faith is to encourage women to grow through their daily work, we must avoid simplistic, restrictive statements about 'women's place'. Many Christian writers suggest that if women feel frustrated as housewives, this is because women's work in the home is undervalued. If they can come to see how important a job it is, they will be satisfied. It is quite true that women's unpaid work is undervalued, but if one is in the wrong occupation, the fact that it is highly valued does not help. Not all women will be suited to serve God and others through a nurturing role; they need freedom to work where their individual talents can best be used.

The loving work of women is something society cannot do without. But we need to be clearer about the meaning of love and service, and we need to acknowledge that women are like other human beings: complex, unique, and very different from one another. I hope that this exploration of what service means and could mean in women's lives will help us to allow God's creative service to flourish more fully in our own lives, whoever we are. As Christians, we want to love our neighbour, but do not always see how. Perhaps Jesus would give us a new parable for today:

> And behold, a Christian stood up to put him to the test, saying 'Teacher, surely you cannot expect me to love others until there is nothing left of me?'
> Jesus replied, 'A woman was making her way through life when she was struck down by chronic arthritis, and she was confined to her home, alone and in pain. Now by chance a government

minister called at the house, and seeing her, went away again quickly. So likewise a deacon, observing her at the window, passed by on the other side. But her next-door-neighbour, hearing her cries through the wall, came into the house and had compassion. Then he too went away again. Later, the woman's daughter called, and took her mother into her own home and cared for her night and day. Which of these, do you think, loved the woman who was disabled?'

'The daughter', said the Christian.

And Jesus said to her, 'Go and do likewise. But those other three must be called back. For it is not right that my daughter should bear this burden of care by herself.'

Notes

Introduction

1. United Nations Report, 1980.
2. W. Somerset Maugham, *The Circle* (Samuel French).
3. A. Atkins, *Split Image* (Hodder and Stoughton 1987); E. Storkey, *What's Right with Feminism* (SPCK, 1985).

1. When he walks through that door

1. Rousseau, quoted in M. Eichler, 'The origin of sex inequality', *Women's Studies International Quarterly* (Vol. 2, No.3, 1979), p. 343.
2. J. Nicholson, *The Heartache of Motherhood* (Sheldon Press 1983), p. 56.
3. A. Gunn, *Mother and Baby* (April 1984), p. 29. See July and August editions for readers' responses.
4. G. Bourne, *Pregnancy* (Pan Books 1983), p. 143.
5. P. King, *How Do You Find the Time?* (Pickering and Inglis 1982), pp. 95–6.
6. ibid., pp. 101–2.
7. J. Dobson, *Man to Man about Women* (Kingsway Publications 1976), p. 73.
8. 'Barbara', quoted in A. Phillips, *Your Body, Your Baby, Your Life* (Pandora 1983), p. 193.
9. See, for example, J. Reeves, *For Better For Worse* (Triangle 1986) and J. Smith, *The Questions Men Ask* (Kingsway Publications 1987).
10. L. Christensen, referred to in E. Storkey, *What's Right with Feminism*, p. 119.
11. Dobson, op. cit., p. 155.
12. King, op. cit., p. 33.
13. K. Brackett, *Mothers and Fathers* (Macmillan 1982).
14. L. McKee, in L. McKee and M. O'Brien (eds.), *The Father Figure* (Tavistock 1982), p. 130.
15. King, op. cit., p. 33.

2. The naturally nicer sex?

1. Michelet, quoted in E. Badinter, *The Myth of Motherhood* (Souvenir Press 1982), p. 215.
2. M. Key, *Male Female Language* (Scarecrow Press, New Jersey, 1975), p. 28.
3. S. Clark, *Man and Woman in Christ* (Servant Books, Michigan, 1980), p. 658.
4. Luther, quoted in E. Morgan, *Thy Humbler Creation* (unpublished 1981), p. 2.
5. John Paul II, *Laborem Exercens* (Catholic Truth Society 1981), p. 71.
6. E. Mitson and others, *Creativity* (Triangle 1985), p. 15.
7. J. Brand, *A Woman's Privilege* (Triangle 1985), p. 53.
8. Dobson, *Man to Man about Women*, p. 174.

9. After H. Anderson, *The Family and Pastoral Care* (Fortress Press, Philadelphia, 1984), pp. 88–9.
10. A. Rich, *Of Woman Born* (Virago 1977), p. 52.
11. S. Goldberg, *The Inevitability of Patriarchy* (Maurice Temple Smith 1977), pp. 194–6.
12. Ruskin, quoted in J.R. Richards, *The Sceptical Feminist* (Routledge and Kegan Paul 1980), p. 125.
13. R. Hamilton, *The Liberation of Women* (George Allen and Unwin 1978). Also see S. Burman (ed.), *Fit Work for Women* (Croom Helm 1979); J. Mitchell and A. Oakley (eds.), *The Rights and Wrongs of Women* (Penguin 1976); and E. Zaretsky, *Capitalism, the Family and Personal Life* (Pluto Press 1976).
14. Hamilton, op. cit., p. 97.
15. Brand, op. cit., p. 40.
16. B. Ehrenreich, *The Hearts of Men* (Pluto 1985).
17. B. Friedan, *The Feminine Mystique* (Penguin 1963).
18. Brand, op. cit., p. 135.
19. For example, see E. Maccoby and C. Jacklin, *The Psychology of Sex Differences* (Stanford University Press 1974); and J. Archer and B. Lloyd, *Sex and Gender* (Penguin, 1982).
20. Richards, op. cit., p. 60.
21. L. Leghorn and K. Parker, *Women's Worth* (Routledge and Kegan Paul 1981), p. 285.

3. The beautiful task of serving

1. A Reformed pastor, quoted in L. Scanzoni and N. Hardesty, *All We're Meant to Be* (Word Books, Texas, 1974) p. 171.
2. R. Ruether, *Mary, the Feminine Face of the Church* (SCM Press 1979), p. 70.
3. Leghorn and Parker, *Women's Worth*, p. 279.
4. R. Ruether, in R. Ruether and E. Bianchi, *From Machismo to Mutuality* (Paulist Press, New York, 1976), pp. 116–17.
5. H. Graham in J. Finch and D. Groves (eds.), *A Labour of Love* (Routledge and Kegan Paul 1983), p. 18.
6. J. B. Miller, *Toward a New Psychology of Women*(Penguin 1983), p. 73.
7. O. Johnston, *Who Needs the Family?* (IVP 1979), p. 113.
8. Smith, *The Questions Men Ask*, p. 56.
9. E. Catherwood, in S. Lees (ed.), *The Role of Women* (IVP, 1984), p. 26.
10. Miller, op.cit., pp. 6ff.
11. ibid., pp.66–7.
12. T. Walter, *All You Love is Need* (SPCK 1985), p. 3.
13. See C. Gilligan, *In a Different Voice* (Harvard University Press 1982) for a discussion of this.
14. J. S. Gummer, *Daily Telegraph* (19 June 1986).
15. Clark, *Man and Woman in Christ*, p. 24.
16. Brand, *A Woman's Privilege*, p. 55.
17. A. Nygren, *Agape and Eros* (SPCK 1932), p. 65.
18. Philippians 2.3–4, 7–8.
19. I Corinthians 13.5–7.
20. A. Whitehouse, in J. McCord and T. Parker (eds.), *Service in Christ* (Epworth 1966), p. 151.
21. A. Richardson, *The Biblical Doctrine of Work* (SCM Press 1963), pp. 41–2.
22. ibid., p. 47.
23. Brand, op. cit., p. 121.

24. King, *How Do You Find the Time?*, p. 100.
25. J. Stott, in Lees (ed.), op. cit., p. 28.

4. *Housewives are human too*

1. J. Milton, *Paradise Lost.*
2. C.P. Gilman, in E. Malos (ed.), *The Politics of Housework* (Allison and Busby 1980), p. 75.
3. See R. Pahl, *Divisions of Labour* (Blackwell 1984), p. 125.
4. A. Coote and B. Campbell, *Sweet Freedom* (Pan Books 1982), p. 81.
5. B. Friedan, *The Feminine Mystique*, p. 211.
6. Smith, *The Questions Men Ask*, p. 104.
7. P. Leach, quoted in D. Hardyment, *Dream Babies* (Oxford University Press 1984), p. 281.
8. See Sharpe *Double Identity* (Penguin 1984), pp. 32 and 37.
9. Equal Opportunities Commission, *Caring for the Elderly and Handicapped* (Manchester 1982).
10. See A. Oakley, *Housewife* (Penguin 1974) and *The Sociology of Housework* (Martin Robertson 1974); and M. Ferree, 'Working-Class Jobs: Housework and Paid Work', *Social Problems* (vol. 23, 1976), pp. 431–441.

5. *Service on the job*

1. E. Stein, quoted in Clark, *Man and Woman in Christ*, p. 392.
2. A woman trade union official, quoted in S. Rowbotham, *Woman's Consciousness, Man's World* (Penguin 1973), p. 97.
3. B. Bryan, S. Dadzie and S. Scafe, *The Heart of the Race* (Virago 1985), p. 25.
4. Kalayaan *Open Space* programme, BBC TV, 1987.
5. This and following quotations are from secretaries interviewed in the *Observer*, 7 November 1982.
6. Rowbotham, op. cit., p. 90.
7. R. Hubbard, M. Henifen and B Fried, *Women Looking at Biology Looking at Women* (G K Hall and Co., Massachusetts, 1979), p. 77.
8. F. Nightingale, quoted in A. Oakley, *Subject Women* (Collins 1981), p. 157.
9. Oakley, op. cit., p. 151.
10. But see Sharpe, *Double Identity*.
11. P. Willis, 'Youth Unemployment 2: Ways of Living', *New Society* (5 April 1984), p. 13.
12. A. Tolson, *The Limits of Masculinity* (Tavistock 1977), pp.35–6.
13. See, for example, J. Carr, *Another Story* (Hamish Hamilton 1984); and D. Tinker, *A Message from the Falklands* (Junction Books 1982).
14. See C. Cooper and M. Davidson, *High Pressure* (Fontana 1982); also A. Borrowdale, 'The Church as an Equal Opportunities Employer', *Crucible* (April 1988).
15. Bryan et al., op. cit., p. 31.
16. See R. Davie, N. Butler and H. Goldstein, *From Birth to Seven* (Longman 1972); M. Rutter, *Maternal Deprivation Reassessed* (Penguin 1972); J. Harper and L. Richards, *Mothers and Working Mothers* (Penguin 1979); and Sharpe, op. cit.

6. Serving without complaint

1. Inchfawn, 1920, quoted in D. Barker and S. Allen, *Dependence and Exploitation in Work and Marriage* (Longman 1976).
2. U. Kroll, *Veils, Mantles, Girdles*, Address to Women in Theology, 10 November 1984.
3. L. Russell in A. Hageman (ed.), *Sexist Religion and Women in the Church* (Association Press 1974), p. 48.
4. King, *How Do You Find the Time?*, p. 21. Original italics omitted.
5. Brand, *A Woman's Privilege*, p. 84.
6. H. Graham in S. Friedman and E. Sarah, *On the Problem of Men* (Women's Press 1982), p. 105.
7. 'Val', in A. Briggs and J. Oliver, *Caring* (Routledge and Kegan Paul 1985), pp. 15–20.
8. D. Soelle, *Suffering* (Darton, Longman and Todd 1975), pp. 103 and 133.
9. A. Campbell, *The Gospel of Anger* (SPCK 1986), p. 50.
10. A. Wilson, *Finding a Voice* (Virago 1978).
11. Miller, *Toward a New Psychology of Women*, p. 61.
12. A. Schaef, *Women's Reality* (Winston Press, Minneapolis, 1985), p. 27.
13. S. Kitzinger, *Women as Mothers* (Fontana 1978), p. 191.
14. Rheingold, quoted in F. Fransella and K. Frost, *On Being a Woman* (Tavistock 1977), p. 158.
15. *Observer*, 5 October 1986.
16. G. Von Rad, *Genesis* (SCM Press 1961), pp. 90–91.
17. Genesis 3.16.
18. B. Harrison, *Work and Worth* (unpublished MA thesis, University of Hull 1983), p. 34.
19. A. Richardson, *Genesis* (SCM Press 1953), p. 75.
20. J. Bowlby, quoted in K. Sylva and I. Lunt, *Child Development* (Basil Blackwell 1982), p. 150.
21. R. Hubbard, in R. Arditti, R. Klein and S. Minden (eds.), *Test-Tube Women* (Pandora Press 1984), p. 342.
22. Harper and Richards, *Mothers and Working Mothers*, p. 30.
23. ibid., pp.111–2.

7. On the receiving end

1. E. Jong, quoted in A. Nilsen et al., (eds.), *Sexism and Language* (NCTE, Illinois, 1977), p. 117.
2. M. Benson, a Victorian woman quoted in Harrison, *Work and Worth*, p. 32.
3. Brand, *A Woman's Privilege*, p. 85.
4. L. Eichenbaum and S. Orbach, *What Do Women Want?* (Fontana 1984), p. 52.
5. See Miller, *Toward a New Psychology of Women*, p. 65.
6. J. Arcana, *Our Mothers' Daughters* (Women's Press 1981), p. 47.
7. See E.E. Morgan, *'The Eroticization of Male Dominance'*, Michigan Papers in Women's Studies (Vol II, no. 1, 1975), pp. 131-2.
8. V. Gornick and B. Moran (eds.), *Woman in Sexist Society* (Basic Books, New York, 1971), p. 92.
9. Reeves, *For Better For Worse*, p. 8.
10. K. Barth, *Church Dogmatics*, vol. III, part 4, (T. and T. Clark 1961), p. 169ff.
11. Rich, *Of Woman Born*, pp. 215-7.
12. H. Cox, *On Not Leaving It to the Snake* (Macmillan 1967), p. ix-xiii.
13. Briggs and Oliver, *Caring*, p. 112.

Notes

14. A. Briggs, in S. Maitland and J. Garcia, (eds.), *Walking on the Water* (Virago 1983), p. 108–10.
15. L. Russell, *Human Liberation in a Feminist Perspective* (Westminster Press, Philadelphia, 1974), p. 144.

8. A love that makes others mature

1. A. Ortlund, *Disciplines of the Beautiful Woman* (Word Publishing 1987), p. 80.
2. H. Oppenheimer, *Incarnation and Innocence* (Hodder and Stoughton 1983), p. 185.
3. W. Vanstone, *Love's Endeavour, Love's Expense* (Darton, Longman and Todd 1977), p. 94.
4. I am here drawing on Oppenheimer's excellent discussion in *The Hope of Happiness* (SCM Press 1983).
5. S. Kierkegaard, quoted in G. Outka, *Agape* (Yale University Press 1972), p. 20.
6. J. Moltmann in E. Moltmann-Wendel and J. Moltmann, *Humanity and God* (SCM Press 1984), p. 122.
7. N. Ferré, in C. Kepley (ed.), *The Theology and Philosophy of Anders Nygren* (Illinois University Press 1970), p. 250–1.
8. E. Moltmann-Wendel, in Moltmann-Wendel and Moltmann, op. cit., p. 120.
9. 'Val', in Briggs and Oliver *Caring*, pp. 16–18.
10. King, *How Do You Find the Time?*, pp. 38–9. Original italics omitted.
11. Richards, *The Sceptical Feminist*, pp. 166-9.
12. ibid., p. 174.
13. Campbell, *The Gospel of Anger*, p. 97.
14. Richardson, *The Biblical Doctrine of Work*.
15. D. Field and E. Stephenson (eds.), *Just the Job* (IVP 1978) p. 76.
16. M. Hebblethwaite, *Motherhood and God* (Geoffrey Chapman 1984), p. 70.

9. Living first for God's sake

1. K. Barth, *Church Dogmatics*, vol. III, part 1, (T. and T. Clark 1956), p. 303.
2. Margaret Fuller, b. 1871, quoted in P. Chesler, *Women and Madness* (Doubleday, New York, 1972), p. 219.
3. Mitson, *Creativity*, p. 13.
4. A. Coates, in Mitson, op. cit., p. 18.
5. P. Brawn, in Mitson, op. cit., p. 105.
6. J. Reeves, in Mitson, op. cit., p. 63.
7. L. Comer, *Wedlocked Women* (Feminist Books 1974), p. 2.
8. P. Brett, *Work and the Theologians* (Church of England Industrial Committee 1979), p. 2.
9. Genesis 1.26–8.
10. J. Oldham, *Work in Modern Society* (SCM Press 1950), p. 22.
11. Brand, *A Woman's Privilege*, p. 82.
12. J. Bernard, *The Future of Marriage* (Souvenir Press 1973), p. 16–7.
13. S. Sharpe, *Just Like a Girl* (Penguin 1976), p. 51.
14. A. Dally, *Why Women Fail* (Wildwood House 1979), pp. 9, 13–14.
15. K. Sakenfeld, 'The Bible and Women', *Theology Today* (vol. 32, 1975), p. 233.
16. H. Catherwood, *The Christian in Industrial Society* (Tyndale Press 1964), p. 2.
17. K. Barth, *Church Dogmatics*, vol. III, part 1, p. 303.
18. Scanzoni and Hardesty, *All We're Meant to Be*, p. 103.
19. L. Russell in Hageman, *Sexist Religion and Women in the Church*, p. 59.
20. Scanzoni and Hardesty, op. cit., p. 206.

21. Matthew 10.34–7.
22. C.S. Lewis, *The Four Loves* (Fontana 1963), p. 114.
23. Eichenbaum and Orbach, *What Do Women Want?*, p. 19.
24. ibid., p. 229.

10. Not nervous of being made happy

1. Ambrose, speaking of headship, quoted in Lees, (ed.), *The Role of Women*, p. 47.
2. S. Callahan, *The Illusion of Eve* (Sheed and Ward, New York, 1965), p. 201.
3. H. Marshall, in Lees (ed.), op.cit., p. 187.
4. Nygren, *Agape and Eros*, p. 170.
5. Oppenheimer, *The Hope of Happiness*, p. 102.
6. ibid., pp. 103–9.
7. Oppenheimer, *The Character of Christian Morality* (Faith Press 1974), p. 95.
8. Brand, *A Woman's Privilege*, p. 57.
9. Russell, *Human Liberation in a Feminist Perspective*, p. 144.
10. Friedan, *The Feminine Mystique*, p. 331.
11. M. Midgley and J. Hughes, *Women's Choices* (Weidenfeld and Nicholson 1983), p. 81.
12. R. Clarke, *Work in Crisis* (The Saint Andrew Press 1982) p. 196.
13. P. Marshall, *Labour of Love* (Wedge Publishing Foundation, Toronto, 1980), p. 16.

Further Reading

Sex Differences
Archer, J. and Lloyd, B. *Sex and Gender*, Penguin 1982.
Nicholson, J. *Men and Women*, Oxford University Press 1984.

Women in Society
Deem, R. *Schooling for Women's Work*, Routledge and Kegan Paul 1980.
Dworkin, A. *Right-Wing Women*, The Women's Press 1983.
Eichenbaum, L. and Orbach, S. *What Do Women Want?*, Fontana 1984.
Gilligan, C. *In a Different Voice*, Harvard University Press 1982.
Miller, J. B. *Toward a New Psychology of Women*, Penguin 1983.
Oakley, A. *Subject Women*, Collins 1981.
Richards, J. R. *The Sceptical Feminist*, Routledge and Kegan Paul 1980.
Sharpe, S. *Just Like a Girl*, Penguin 1976.
Taylor, D. et al. *Women: A World Report*, Methuen 1985.

Black Women's Experience
Bryan, B., Dadzie, S. and Scafe, S. *The Heart of the Race*, Virago 1985.
Wilson, A. *Finding a Voice*, Virago 1978.

Women in Employment
Aldred, C. *Women at Work*, Pan Books 1981.
Coyle, A. *Redundant Women*, The Women's Press 1984.
Sharpe, S. *Double Identity*, Penguin 1984.
West, J., ed., *Work, Women and the Labour Market*, Routledge and Kegan Paul 1982.
Westwood, S. *All Day Every Day*, Pluto 1984.

Women in the Home
Bernard, J. *The Future of Marriage*, Souvenir Press 1973.
Finch, J. *Married to the Job*, George Allen and Unwin 1983.
Friedan, B. *The Feminine Mystique*, Penguin 1963.
Friedan, B. *The Second Stage*, New York, Summit Books, 1981.
Oakley, A. *Housewife*, Penguin 1974.
Piotrkowski, C. *Work and the Family System*, New York, The Free Press, 1978.
Sanders, D. with Reed, J. *Kitchen Sink or Swim?*, Penguin 1982.

Mothering
Backett, K. *Mothers and Fathers*, Macmillan 1982.
Boulton, M. *On Being a Mother*, Tavistock 1984.

Harper, J. and Richards, L. *Mothers and Working Mothers*, Penguin 1979.
Nicholson, J. *The Heartache of Motherhood*, Sheldon Press 1983.
Rich, A. *Of Woman Born*, Virago 1977.
Schaffer, R. *Mothering*, Fontana 1977.

Caring
Briggs, A. and Oliver, J. *Caring*, Routledge and Kegan Paul 1985.
Finch, J. and Groves, D., eds., *A Labour of Love*, Routledge and Kegan Paul 1983.

Christian Reflection on Women and the Family
Anderson, H. *The Family and Pastoral Care*, Philadelphia, Fortress Press 1984.
Green, W. *The Future of the Family*, Mowbray 1984.
Hebblethwaite, M. *Motherhood and God*, Geoffrey Chapman 1984.

Women and Christianity
Atkins, A. *Split Image*, Hodder and Stoughton 1987.
Byrne, L. *Women before God*, SPCK 1988.
Dawson, R. *And All that is Unseen*, Church House Publishing 1986.
Dowell, S. and Hurcombe, L. *Dispossessed Daughters of Eve*, SPCK 1987.
Furlong, M., ed., *Mirror to the Church*, SPCK 1988.
Garcia, J. and Maitland, S., eds., *Walking on the Water*, Virago 1983.
Loades, A. *Searching for Lost Coins*, SPCK 1987.
Russell, L. *Human Liberation in a Feminist Perspective*, Philadelphia, Westminster Press, 1974.
Scanzoni, L.and Hardesty, N. *All We're Meant to Be*, Word Books, Texas, 1974.
Storkey, E. *What's Right with Feminism*, SPCK 1985.

Theological Reflection on Work and Service
Campbell, A. *The Gospel of Anger*, SPCK 1986.
Clarke, R. *Work in Crisis*, The Saint Andrew Press 1982.
Oppenheimer, H. *The Hope of Happiness*, SCM 1983.
Soelle, D. with Cloyes, S. A. *To Work and to Love*, Philadelphia, Fortress Press, 1984.
Vanstone, W. *Love's Endeavour, Love's Expense*, Darton, Longman and Todd 1977.

Men and Service
Ehrenreich, B. *The Hearts of Men*, Pluto 1985.
Tinker, D. *A Message from the Falklands*, Junction Books 1982.
Tolson, A. *The Limits of Masculinity*, Tavistock 1977.